D0745027

BAG OF TRICKS

Photocopy Handouts for Regular and Substitute ESL Teachers

Paul J. Hamel

ACKNOWLEDGEMENTS

Grateful acknowledgements are due to George Gati for contributing two stories and editing. Thanks also goes to Nancy Loncke for inspiring two lessons; Harriett Rose, Susan Wilson, and Wanda Perry for editing and proofreading; and Richard Patchin for his support, valuable ideas, and insights.

ISBN 0–937354–20–1
First published in 1991 by Delta Systems Co., Inc.
570 Rock Road Drive
Dundee, IL 60118

Printed in the United States of America

Table of Contents

Introduction

- Ever substitute in an ESL class, and the regular teacher didn't leave you a lesson plan?

- Ever find that if the teacher did leave you a lesson plan, it was either illegible, skimpy, or unclear?

- Does your regular ESL textbook need supplementing?

- Need a little help?

If so, BAG OF TRICKS is for you.

The lessons in BAG OF TRICKS are blackline masters designed to be photocopied and distributed to students. Clear, detailed lesson plans accompany each lesson.

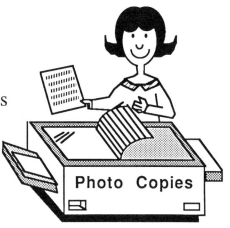

BAG OF TRICKS is organized by level of difficulty. It is a collection of lessons that covers a diverse range of topics and key grammatical structures.

- Use the lessons to make overhead transparencies.

- Give them as homework assignments.

- Use them to reinforce your regular lessons.

- Add them to YOUR "bag of tricks."

- Give them to YOUR next substitute!

Beginning
Level

1 Student Mixer

Directions: *Walk around the room and find the students with the information below. Then, write the students' names on the lines.*

1 _____ has a job.

2 _____ doesn't work.

3 _____ has a brother.

4 _____ has a sister.

5 _____ takes the bus.

6 _____ doesn't speak my language.

7 _____ lives near school.

8 _____ is handsome.

9 _____ is pretty.

10 _____ drives a car.

11 _____ doesn't smoke.

12 _____ is a good student.

2

BAG OF TRICKS by Paul J. Hamel, © 1990 Delta Systems Co., Inc.

1 Review all the vocabulary:

is	brother	live	drive
has	sister	language	car
doesn't	bus	near	smoke
job	school	handsome	good
work	speak	pretty	student

2 Review the following phrases:

What's your name?
Please spell it.
Do you ... ?
Are you ... ?
Who is ... ?
Who ... + (present tense) ?
Does he/she ... ?
Is he/she ...?

3 Read the directions at the top of the handout with the students.

Use this group activity as a "mixer" exercise in which students have to talk to each other to get the necessary information. Have students get up and walk around the room to collect the names of other students who match the description on the handout. Allow at least 15 minutes. This is an excellent way for students to get to know one another especially at the beginning of a new term.

4 Have students practice asking and answering questions about the information collected.

Who has a ... ?
Who doesn't ... ?
Who is ... ?

5 Follow-up by having the class make up an additional list of other kinds of personal information (i.e., is married, is single, has children, can sing, etc.) and repeat the exercise.

2 Imperative: do & don't

1 *Help Daniel decide. Write "Do it!" or "Don't do it!"*

DON'T DO IT!

DO IT!

Daniel

1. Eat in the classroom.
2. Listen to the teacher.
3. Write on the desks.
4. Make noise.
5. Take a break.
6. Correct your mistakes.
7. Be careful.
8. Do your homework.
9. Forget your book.
10. Help the teacher.
11. Come to school.
12. Sit on the desk.
13. Erase the chalkboard.
14. Take a test.
15. Go home.

Don't do it!
Do it!

Review the meanings of the commands on the handout.

Write on the walls.	Correct your mistakes.	Come to school.
Listen to the teacher.	Be careful.	Sit on the desk.
Write on the desks.	Do your homework.	Erase the chalkboard.
Make noise.	Forget your book.	Take a test.
Take a break.	Help the teacher.	Go home.

❷ Teach the meaning of "Do it!" and "Don't do it!" Then drill the students orally.

❸ Explain how to fill in the sentences "Do it!" and "Don't do it!" (See examples.)
Read the directions and do a few examples with the whole class. Correct the
exercise and ask students to think of more situations. Write them on the
chalkboard.

❹ Expand the exercise by doing an oral drill using the following mini-dialog, the
commands on the handout, and additional commands below.

Student #1: Hold it!
Student #2: What's the matter?
Student #1: Don't .... or ....(imperative form).......!

1. open the windows
2. close the door
3. run in the hall
4. pick up the table
5. drink in the classroom
6. smoke in school
7. throw away the trash
8. chew gum
9. eat in class
10. write on the walls

❺ As a follow-up activity, play a pantomime game. Divide the class into two
teams. Have members of the teams take turns acting out a series of actions.
The opposite team must guess the actions. Keep count of each team's correct
guesses.

 As an additional follow-up activity, teach other expressions in the imperative:

1. Take care!
2. Watch out!
3. Look out!
4. Don't do that!
5. Wait!
6. Stop!
7. Keep out!
8. Do not enter!
9. Handle with care!
10. Do not inhale!

5

3 Prepositions

1 *Draw the items listed below in the picture.*

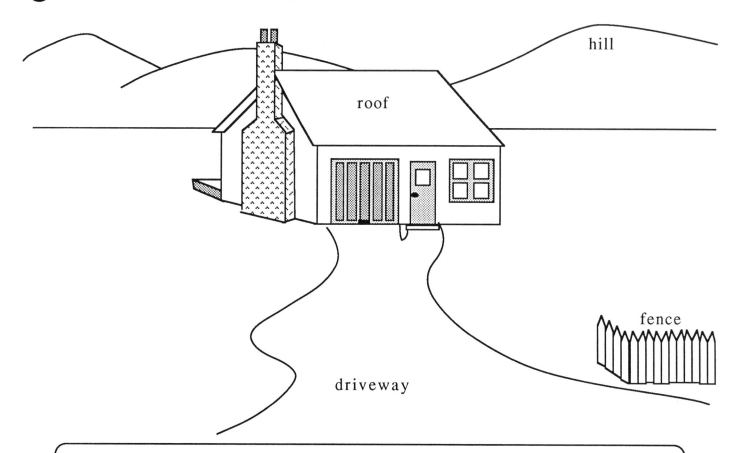

1. Draw a car <u>in</u> the driveway.
2. Draw a bicycle <u>next to</u> the car.
3. Draw a tall tree in front of the house.
4. Draw a bush <u>to the right of</u> the house.
5. Draw a cat <u>on</u> the roof.
6. Draw a table <u>with</u> an umbrella <u>to the left of</u> the house.
7. Draw two chairs <u>behind</u> the table.
8. Draw a dog <u>under</u> the table.
9. Draw a fence <u>around</u> the house.
10. Draw flowers <u>between</u> the fence and the house.
11. Draw clouds <u>over</u> the house.
12. Draw ....

2 *Color the objects. Example: "Color the car blue."*

 <u>BAG OF TRICKS</u> by Paul J. Hamel, © 1990 Delta Systems Co., Inc.

1 Directions

• Review the use of common prepositions, adjectives, nouns, and word order. Have the students not only describe where to draw an item but also how it should look.

• Project a copy of the handout on an overhead transparency directly onto the chalkboard where the students can draw the picture. You may want to use colored chalk to make the activity more interesting.

• Have students read commands beginning with the word "draw." Continue the activity by having students give original commands. A typical dialog should sound something like the following:

> Student: Please draw a car.
> Teacher: Where?
> Student: In the driveway.
> Teacher: Please repeat.
> Student: Please draw a car in the driveway.
> Teacher: Near the house or far from the house?
> Student: Near the house.
> Teacher: Please say it all.
> Student: Please draw a car on the driveway near the house.
> Teacher: What kind of car?
> Student: A big car.
> Teacher: Please say it all.
> Student: Please draw a big car on the driveway near the house.
> Teacher: What color?
> Student: White.
> Teacher: Please say it all.
> Student: Please draw a big white car on the driveway near the house.

• Continue the exercise by having volunteers take turns drawing items in the scene on the chalkboard.

2 Reverse the exercise by having the students erase all the items one at a time until nothing is left on the chalkboard.

Example:

Student #1: Please erase the car in the picture.
Student #2: Where is it?
Student #1: It's in front of the house.

7

4 Using Social Language

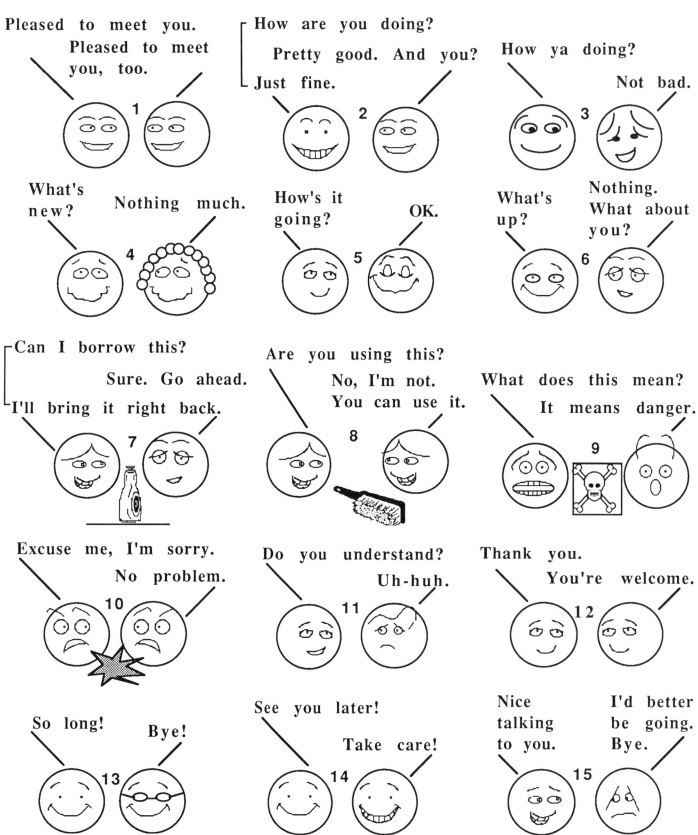

Pleased to meet you.
Pleased to meet you, too.
1

How are you doing?
Pretty good. And you?
Just fine.
2

How ya doing?
Not bad.
3

What's new?
Nothing much.
4

How's it going?
OK.
5

What's up?
Nothing. What about you?
6

Can I borrow this?
Sure. Go ahead.
I'll bring it right back.
7

Are you using this?
No, I'm not. You can use it.
8

What does this mean?
It means danger.
9

Excuse me, I'm sorry.
No problem.
10

Do you understand?
Uh-huh.
11

Thank you.
You're welcome.
12

So long!
Bye!
13

See you later!
Take care!
14

Nice talking to you.
I'd better be going. Bye.
15

8

1 Directions

• Teach the fifteen mini-dialogs with actions. Use as much non verbal communication as possible to show the correct context of each mini-dialog (e.g., shaking hands while saying, "Pleased to meet you").

• Have the whole class repeat each line of the mini-dialogs after you have modeled the sentences. Break up longer sentences into segments, or use a backward-buildup technique, starting at the end of the sentence and working toward the beginning. Here is a demonstration of the technique.

Instructor	*Student*
going.	going.
be going.	be going.
better be going.	better be going.
I'd better be going.	I'd better be going.

• Teach the second line (the rejoinder) in the same manner. Repeat the first line and have a student respond with the rejoinder. Then reverse roles.

• Select two students to repeat the two lines. Continue with a chain drill in which one student asks a question or makes a statement and another student makes an appropriate rejoinder.

• Have the students practice the dialog(s) in pairs.

• Using an overhead projector or chalkboard, help the students write several of the mini-dialogs to create several longer ones. Then encourage the students to present the new dialogs in front of the class.

• Encourage students to write their own 8-line dialog using some of the expressions and vocabulary in the lesson.

2 Follow-up Activities

• Write the first part of the rejoinder on the chalkboard and have the students come up to write the second part.

• Give several mini-dialogs as a dictation on a subsequent day.

5 Forming Plurals

Directions

1. Study the rules for forming the plural.

2. Write the words in the singular or plural with "the."
Use the words below.

Vocabulary

clock	door
chalkboard	pen
direction	map
window	dog
woman	chair
person	book

Spelling Rules

• Add "s" to most words.

one (1) pencil

two (2) pencils

• Add "es" after "s," "sh," "ch," "z," and "x" (/ks/).

one dress

two dresses

one box

two boxes

Exceptions

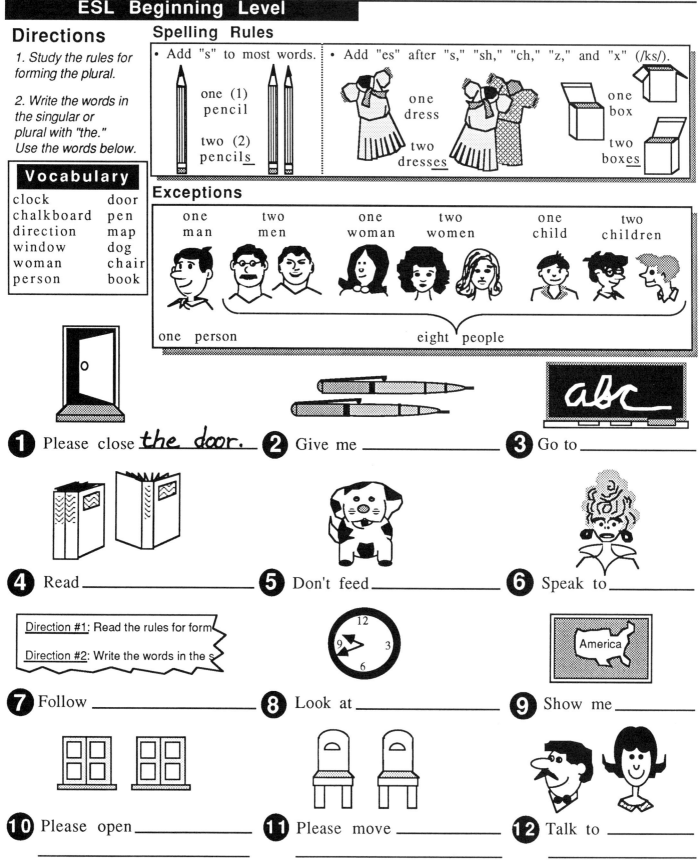

one man · two men · one woman · two women · one child · two children

one person · eight people

1 Please close *the door.*

2 Give me _____

3 Go to _____

4 Read _____

5 Don't feed _____

6 Speak to _____

Direction #1: Read the rules for form

Direction #2: Write the words in the s

7 Follow _____

8 Look at _____

9 Show me _____

10 Please open _____

11 Please move _____

12 Talk to _____

10

1 Teach the names of the items on the handout. (See Vocabulary in the box.) Then teach the verb commands (imperative): close, give, go, read, feed, speak, open, move, talk. Also teach the words "don't" and "please."

• Explain the rules for forming the plural of nouns in the boxes at the top of the page.

• Use the exercise as an oral drill. (Discourage students from writing. This should be a time for oral practice.) Make sure that the students use the article "the" in front of each noun.

• After the students have sufficiently practiced the commands orally, have them write the correct word, singular or plural, on the line provided. Remind students to write "the" in front of each noun.

Answers:

1. Please close the door.	5. Don't feed the dog.	9. Show me the map.
2. Give me the pens.	6. Speak to the woman.	10. Please open the windows.
3. Go to the chalkboard.	7. Follow the directions.	11. Please move the chairs.
4. Read the books.	8. Look at the clock.	12. Talk to the people.

2 Practice the pronunciation of the plural endings. Tell the students that we pronounce the "s" and "es" three ways:
• After unvoiced consonants /s/
• After voiced consonants /z/
• After /s/, /sh/, /ch/, /ks/ (written as "x") sounds pronounce "es" as /iz/

Have students practice the following words:

/ s /	/z/	/iz/
books	chairs	dresses
lamps	pens	glasses
students	windows	businesses
maps	schools	dishes
streets	pictures	boxes
sports	cars	houses
immigrants	numbers	watches
shops	doors	classes
maps	rooms	buses
clocks	pencils	churches

3 On a subsequent day, teach the formation of the plural of words that end in "y" (/ee/ sound): change the "y" to "i" and add "es."
Examples:

party-parties	fly-flies
country-countries	cherry-cherries
dictionary-dictionaries	family-families
baby-babies	body-bodies

Note the exceptions: day-days, toy-toys, boy-boys.

4 As a follow-up activity, play "Simon Says." Have the students stand up. Tell them that they have to do whatever you tell them to do except when you do not begin the command with the words "Simon Says." Students who do so are eliminated from the game and have to sit down.

6 Body Parts

1 *Study the parts of the body.*

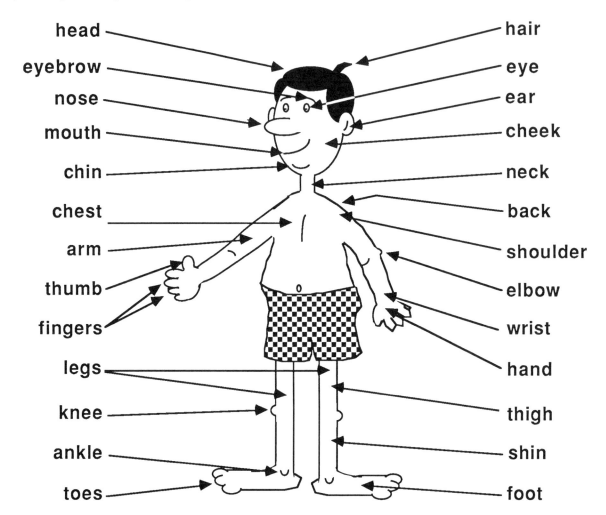

head · hair · eyebrow · eye · nose · ear · mouth · cheek · chin · neck · chest · back · arm · shoulder · thumb · elbow · fingers · wrist · legs · hand · knee · thigh · ankle · shin · toes · foot

2 PAIR PRACTICE

Talk with another student. Use the picture.

Student 1: Where does it hurt ....?
Student 2: My .... hurts.

Use the picture above.

Student 1: What's the matter?
Student 2: I have a pain in my ....

Where does it hurt?

My left hand hurts.

What's the matter?

I have a pain in my right leg.

   BAG OF TRICKS by Paul J. Hamel, © 1990 Delta Systems Co., Inc.

1 Read and explain the different parts of the body. Practice the pronunciation of the vocabulary. Then, have volunteers go to the chalkboard and draw parts of the body. As they draw a part, they have to name it.

• Play "Simon Says." Have all the students stand up. The leader says, "Simon says to touch your ... ." The students have to obey. If the order is not preceded by the words "Simon says," then the students must not move. If they do, they are out of the game and have to sit down. The person who remains standing wins. Make the game more challenging by having the leader touch one part of the body, but call a different part of the body.

2 Using an overhead transparency, practice the pair practice exercises as whole-class oral drills.

• After the students are familiar with the phrases, have them do the pair practice exercises. Pairing exercises give the students time, especially in large classes, to practice important speaking skills. Have each student choose a partner. (The first few times, you will probably have to go around the classroom and pair up students.) Encourage the students to pair up with different partners each time. While students are doing the exercise, walk around the room, listen to individuals, and correct mistakes.

3 As a follow-up exercise, you might want to teach some additional body parts:

Body	Hand	Head	Eye	Foot
face	knuckle	sideburn	eyelid	heel
forhead	fingernail	nostril	eyelashes	instep
armpit	index finger	beard	iris	ball
waist	middle finger	mustache	pupil	big toe
abdomen	ring finger	tongue		little toe
buttocks	little finger	tooth		toenail
hip	palm	lip		
calf				

13

7 Student Mixer: Clothes

ESL Beginning Level

Directions: Walk around the room and find the students with the clothes below. Write the students' names on the lines.

1 _____ is wearing brown shoes.

2 _____ is wearing a long-sleeved shirt.

3 _____ is wearing a black belt.

4 _____ is wearing a jacket.

5 _____ is wearing green socks.

6 _____ is wearing a skirt.

7 _____ is wearing glasses.

8 _____ is wearing a short-sleeved shirt.

9 _____ is wearing a blouse.

10 _____ is wearing a tie.

11 _____ is wearing tennis shoes.

12 _____ is wearing blue pants.

14

BAG OF TRICKS by Paul J. Hamel, © 1990 Delta Systems Co., Inc.

1 Review all the vocabulary:

shoes	shirt	tennis shoes	green
shirt	glasses	long-sleeved	blue
belt	blouse	short-sleeved	wear
jacket	tie	brown	
socks	pants	black	

2 Review the following phrases:

What's your name? Please spell it.
What are you wearing?
Are you wearing ... ?
Who is wearing a ... ?
Who has a ... ?
What color is/are the ... ?
What kind of ... are you wearing?

3 Language Activity

Read the directions at the top of the handout with the students.

• Use this group activity as a "mixer" exercise in which students have to talk to each other to get the necessary information. Have students get up and walk around the room to collect the names of other students who match the clothes description on the handout. Allow 15 minutes. This is an excellent way for students to get to know one another especially at the beginning of a new term.

• Have students practice asking and answering questions about the information collected.

Who is wearing ... ? (Introduce the words: "nobody" or "no one" if necessary.)
Who has a ... at home?
What color is your ... ?

4 Follow-up Activity

Practice the general sequence of adjectives: 1. size   2. color   3. noun

Examples: small white shirt; short blue skirt; long black belt   15

8 His, Her, Their

Pair Practice *Practice the question and answers with another student.*

Example

Whose key is it?

It's his key.

Clara
Alex
his   her
their

Alex
key

1 *It's his key.*

handbag
Clara

2 _____

Alex and Clara

3 _____

Alex
shoes

4 _____

ALEX
shirt

5 _____

Alex and Clara
son

6 _____

Clara
blouse

7 _____

CHECK
...Clara...

8 _____

picture

9 _____

present
Alex

10 _____

Alex and Clara
house

11 _____

To Alex
letter

12 _____

Alex
Diary   book

13 _____

Clara
Perfume

14 _____

tie
Alex

15 _____

Alex and Clara
pets

16 _____

Write *Practice writing sentences with "his," "her," or "their" below the pictures.*

16

1 Read the names of the people (Alex and Clara) in the box to the right. Then identify and pronounce the names of the items on the handouts. Then, read and practice the question and answer in the speech balloons. "Whose key is it?" and "It's his key." Continue the drill substituting the items in the pictures. (Discourage students from writing. This should be a time for oral practice.) Continue the substitution drill by pointing to items in the room.

Pair students and have them practice the drill again orally.

Have students write sentences with "his," "her," and "their" below each picture.

Correct the sentences. You may want to project a copy of the handout that has been transfered to an overhead transparency directly onto a chalkboard where students can write the correct answers.

2 Follow-Up

• Practice the use of possessive case using "'s" and the names "Alex" and "Clara." Example: "Whose key is it?"   "It's Alex's key."

• Review the use of object pronouns (me, you, him, her, it, us, them). Practice the expression "belong to."
Example: "Whose key does it belong to?"   "It belongs to him."

• Contrast possessive pronouns with possessive adjectives (my, your, his, her, our, its, their). Try to use real items.
Example: "This is my key. Please give it to me."
          "This is her bag. Please give it to her."
          "These are his shoes. Please give them to him."

• For a more advanced group, teach the use of possessive pronouns (mine, his, hers, its, ours, theirs). Example:
          "Whose is it?" (Point to a bag.)   "It's hers." (Point to a woman.)
          "Whose are they? (Point to shoes.)   "They're his" (Point to a man.)

Answers

1. It's his key.	7. It's her blouse.	13. It's his book.
2. It's her handbag.	8. It's her check.	14. It's her perfume.
3. It's their car.	9. It's her picture.	15. It's his tie.
4. They're his shoes.	10. It's his present.	16. They're their pets.
5. It's his shirt.	11. It's their house.	
6. He's their son.	12. It's his letter.	

17

9 The Possessive ('s)

Pair Practice *Practice the question and answers orally with another student.*

Example

Whose cup is it?

It's Helen's cup.

1 Whose cup is it?   Helen

It's Helen's cup.

2 Whose pencil is it?

_____ Peter

3 Whose handbag is it?   Judy

_____

4 Whose picture is it?

_____ Jimmy

5 Whose books are they?   Paul

_____

6 Whose bones are they?   dog

_____

7 Whose car is it?   Miss Bartel

_____

8 Whose bags are they?   DURAN

_____

9 Whose home is it?   Sencer

_____

10 Whose restaurant is it?   JOE

_____

11 Whose office is it?   DENTIST

_____

12 Whose office is it?   DOCTOR

_____

Write *Practice writing sentences with the possessive case ('s) next to the pictures.*

18   <u>BAG OF TRICKS</u> by Paul J. Hamel, © 1990 Delta Systems Co., Inc.

1 Identify and pronounce the names of the people and items on the handouts. Read and practice the question and answer in the speech balloons. "Whose cup is it?" and "It's Helen's cup." Continue the drill substituting the items in the pictures. (Discourage students from writing. This should be a time for oral practice.) Continue the substitution drill by pointing to items in the room.

Pair students and have them practice the drill again orally.

2 Have students write sentences with the possessive ('s) beside each picture.

Correct the sentences. You may want to project a copy of the handout that has been transfered to an overhead transparency directly onto a chalkboard where students can write the correct answers.

3 Follow-Up

• Practice the use of possessive adjectives (his, her, their).
"Clara." Example: "Whose cup is it?"   "It's <u>her</u> cup."

• Practice the use of the expression "belong to."
Example: "Whose cup does it <u>belong to?</u>"   "It belongs to <u>Helen.</u>"

• Review the use of object pronouns (me, you, him, her, it, us, them) with the expression "belong to."
Example: "Whose cup does it <u>belong to?</u>"   "It belongs to <u>her.</u>" (Point to Helen.)

• Contrast possessive pronouns with possessive adjectives (my, your, his, her, our, its, their). Try to use real items.
Example: "This is <u>my</u> pen. It belongs to <u>me.</u>"
          "This is <u>her</u> bag. It belongs to <u>her.</u>"
          "These are <u>his</u> shoes. They belong to <u>him.</u>"

• Practice the short form of the possessive.
Example: "Whose cup is it?" "It's Helen's cup."
          "Excuse me, <u>whose?</u>"   "<u>Helen's.</u>"

Answers

1. It's Helen's cup.	7. It's Miss Bartel's car.
2. It's Peter's pencil.	8. They're Duran's bags.
3. It's Judy's handbag.	9. It's Sencer's home.
4. It's Jimmy's picture.	10. It's Joe's restaurant.
5. They're Paul's books.	11. It's a dentist's office.
6. They're the dog's bones.	12. It's a doctor's office.

19

10 Telling Time

READ *Practice reading the time.*

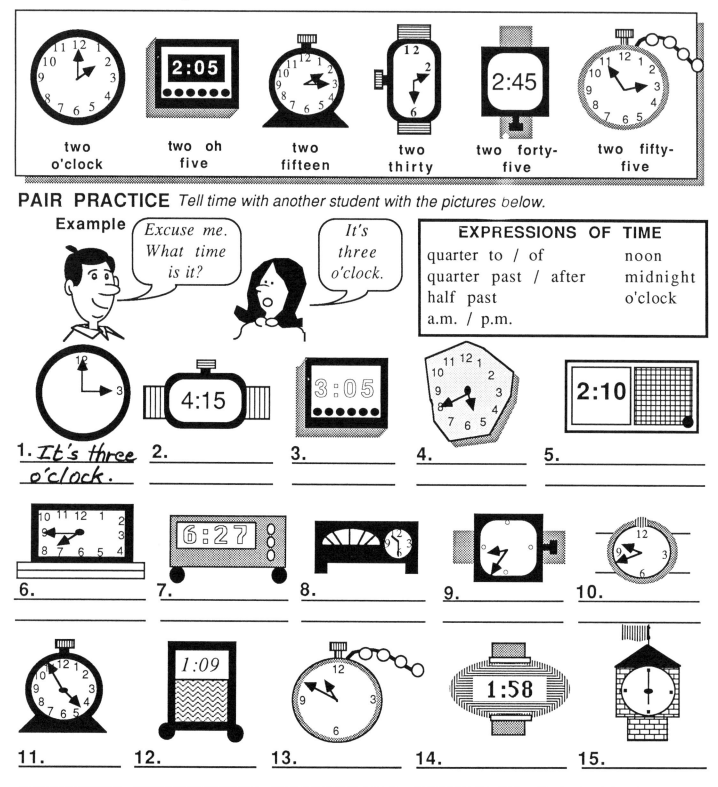

two o'clock	two oh five	two fifteen	two thirty	two forty-five	two fifty-five

PAIR PRACTICE *Tell time with another student with the pictures below.*

Example

Excuse me. What time is it?

It's three o'clock.

EXPRESSIONS OF TIME

quarter to / of   noon
quarter past / after   midnight
half past   o'clock
a.m. / p.m.

4:15

3:05

2:10

1. *It's three o'clock.*
2. _____
3. _____
4. _____
5. _____

6:27

6. _____
7. _____
8. _____
9. _____
10. _____

1:09

1:58

11. _____
12. _____
13. _____
14. _____
15. _____

WRITE *Practice writing the time in words below the pictures.*

   BAG OF TRICKS by Paul J. Hamel, © 1990 Delta Systems Co., Inc.

Pair Practice / Fill In

1 Read the time on the clocks and watches in the box at the top of the page. (Point out the difference between "clock" and "watch".) Then, read and practice the question and answer in the speech balloon in the Pair Practice exercise: "Excuse me. What time is it?" and "It's three o'clock." Continue the drill substituting the times in the pictures. (Discourage students from writing. This should be a time for oral practice.) Continue the substitution drill with different times by using a real clock or drawings on a chalkboard.

2 Pair students and have them practice the drill again orally.

3 Have students write sentences indicating the time below each watch or clock.

Correct the sentences. You may want to project a copy of the handout that has been transfered to an overhead transparency directly onto a chalkboard where students can write and see the correct answers.

Answers:

1. Three o'clock.	6. Seven forty-five.	11. Four fifty-five.
2. Four fifteen.	7. Six twenty-seven.	12. One oh nine.
3. Three oh five.	8. Eleven thirty.	13. Ten fifty.
4. Five forty.	9. Eight thirty-five.	14. Six fifty-nine.
5. Two ten.	10. Nine forty.	15. Six o'clock.

4 Teach the other expressions of time (see box):

quarter to	half past	midnight
quarter of	a.m. (ante meridiem)	o'clock
quarter past	p.m. (post meridiem)	
quarter after	noon	

5 Repeat the oral and written exercises again using the new expressions of time. Answers:

1. Three o'clock.	6. Quarter to eight.	11. Five to five.
2. Quarter past four.	7. Twenty-seven past six.	12. Nine past one.
3. Five past three.	8. Half past ten.	13. Ten to eleven.
4. Twenty to six.	9. Twenty-five to nine.	14. Two to two.
5. Ten past two.	10. Twenty to ten.	15. Six o'clock.

21

11 Money

1 *Pronounce the names of the coins and read the note in the boxes below.*

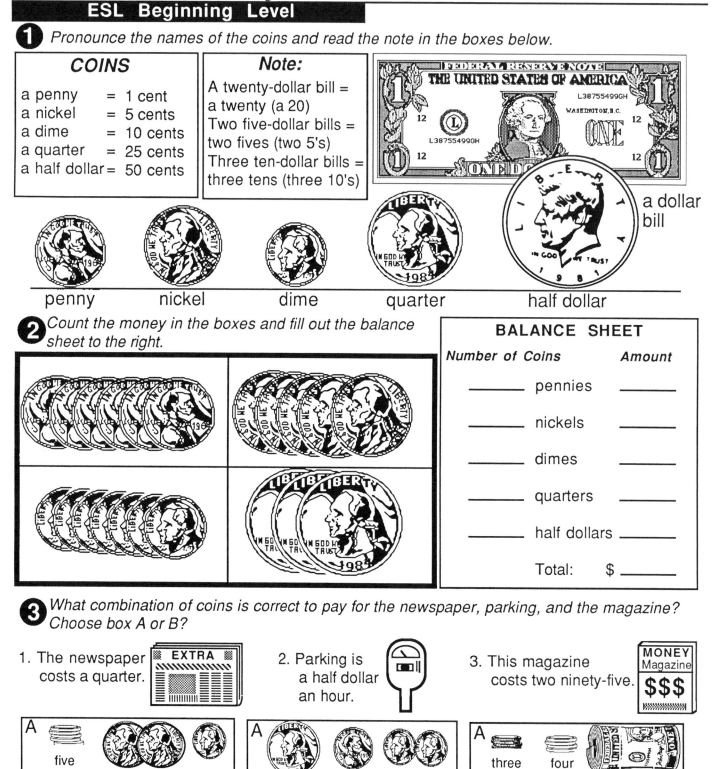

COINS

a penny   = 1 cent
a nickel = 5 cents
a dime   = 10 cents
a quarter = 25 cents
a half dollar = 50 cents

Note:

A twenty-dollar bill =
a twenty (a 20)
Two five-dollar bills =
two fives (two 5's)
Three ten-dollar bills =
three tens (three 10's)

a dollar bill

penny   nickel   dime   quarter   half dollar

2 *Count the money in the boxes and fill out the balance sheet to the right.*

BALANCE SHEET

Number of Coins		Amount
_____	pennies	_____
_____	nickels	_____
_____	dimes	_____
_____	quarters	_____
_____	half dollars	_____
	Total:	$ _____

3 *What combination of coins is correct to pay for the newspaper, parking, and the magazine? Choose box A or B?*

1. The newspaper costs a quarter.   **EXTRA**

2. Parking is a half dollar an hour.

3. This magazine costs two ninety-five.   **MONEY Magazine** $$$

A five pennies   two nickels   a dime

B a dime   two nickels   a penny

A a quarter   a penny   two dimes

B a quarter   a quarter

A three quarters   four nickels   two dollars

B seven quarters   one dollar

1
- Distribute the handout and pronounce the names of the coins and bills. (If possible, bring actual coins and pass them around in the class.)
- Read and explain the information in the note.
- Practice the names of the coins by doing a simple drill:

    Student #1: *How much is a ___(penny)___ and a ___(nickel)___?*
    Student #2: *It's ___(six)___ cents.*

- Practice the use of the short form for bills:

    Student #1: *How much are ___(2 tens)___ and ___(3 fives)___?*
    Student #2: ___(35)___ *dollars.*

- Do an additional drill:

    Student #1: *Can you change a ___(20 or twenty dollar bill)___?*
    Student #2: *Yes, I can. Here you are.*
                    or
    No, I can't. I only have ___(2 fives)___.

2
- Read the directions and ask the students to fill out the balance sheet.

- You may want to project a copy of the handout that has been transferred to an overhead transparency directly onto the chalkboard where students can write the correct answers.

- Teach the names of the symbols for the following: + plus, - minus, and = equals (or "is.")

- Practice using the symbols +, -, and = by having students count the money they have in their pockets or purses.

3
- As a reading comprehension exercise, read the directions with the students and have them choose which of the two choices are correct: box A or B.

ANSWERS

ANSWERS

BALANCE SHEET		
Number of Coins		*Amount*
6	pennies	.06
5	nickels	.25
7	dimes	.70
3	quarters	.75
0	half dollars	0
	Total:	$ 1.76

1. A (Five pennies, two nickels, and a dime equal twenty-five cents or a quarter.)
2. B (Two quarters equal 50 cents or a half dollar.)
3. A (Three quarters, four nickels, and two dollars equal two dollars and ninety-five cents or two ninety-five.)

- Challenge: Name the people on U.S. bills.

12 Simple Present does & doesn't

1 *Read the story about Bob and Tom.*

Bob

Bob lives in California.
Tom lives in New York.
Bob rents a house.
Tom rents an apartment.
Bob works outside.
Tom works in an office.
Bob drives a truck.
Tom drives a car.

Tom

2 *Write the missing words.*

1. Bob _lives_ in California; he _doesn't_ _live_ in New York.
2. Bob _____ a house; he_____ _____ an apartment.
3. Bob _____ outside; he _____ _____ in an office.
4. Bob _____ a truck; he _____ _____ a car.

5._____Bob _____ in California? _____, he _____.
6._____Bob _____ an apartment? _____, he _____.
7._____Bob _____ outside? _____, he _____.
8._____Bob _____ a car? _____, he _____.
9._____Bob _____ a truck? _____, he _____.
10._____Bob _____ in New York? _____, he _____.

3 *Read the story about Mary and Nancy.*

Nancy

Nancy lives in Chicago.
Mary lives in Miami.
Nancy works in a store.
Mary works in a factory.
Nancy eats lunch at home.
Mary eats lunch at work.

Mary

4 *Write the missing words.*

11. Nancy _____ in Chicago; she_____ _____ in Miami.
12. Mary _____ in Miami; she_____ _____ in Chicago.
13. Nancy _____ in a store; she_____ _____ in a factory.
14. Mary _____ lunch at work; she _____ _____ at home.

15._____Nancy _____ in Chicago? _____, she _____.
16._____Nancy _____ in Miami? _____, she _____.
17._____Nancy _____ in a store? _____, she _____.
18._____Nancy _____ at work? _____, she _____.

24

1 Before distributing a copy of the handout, read the story about Bob and Tom to the students as a listening comprehension exercise. Then ask simple "yes/ no" comprehension questions using "does." Example: Question: "Does Bob live in California?" Have students answer "Yes, he does," or "No, he doesn't."

Distribute the handouts and read the stories again while the students underline unfamiliar vocabulary. Then explain the vocabulary. (You might want to project the story onto a screen or chalkboard using an overhead projector.) Point out the "s" at the end of each verb.

2 Use the fill-in exercises in section 2 as oral drills. (Discourage students from writing. This should be a time for oral practice.) Continue the drill by having students ask questions using "does."

3 Next, have students write in the missing words. (See handwritten examples.)

Correct the sentences. You may want to project a copy of the handout that has been transfered to an overhead transparency directly onto a chalkboard where students can write and see the correct answers.

4 Repeat the same procedure for sections 3 and 4.

Follow-Up

• As a class, write a six-line text about two students in your class modeled on the stories on the handout. Practice asking and answering about the new story using "does" and doesn't."

• Explain the spelling rules for the third person singular ending:
   1. add "-es" to verbs that end with "s," "sh," "ch," "z," and "x" sounds.
   2. when words end in "y" preceded by a consonant, change the "y" to "i" and add "-es." This is the same rule for forming plural nouns.
   3. add "-s" to most other verbs.
   Examples:
   She punches in at 8 a.m. She finishes at 5 p.m. He studies in the evening.
   (Other verbs: change, catch, teach, wash, watch, dress, miss, marry, study)

• Locate Hollywood, New York, Miami, and Chicago on a map.

• On a subsequent day, give the stories as a dictation.

13 Simple Present: do & don't

1 *Read the story about George and Will.*

George and Will like sports.
They play baseball. They play football.
They play basketball.
They don't play soccer. They don't play hockey.

2 *Write the missing words.*

1. __Do__ George and Will play baseball?   __yes,__ they __do__.
2. __Do__ George and Will play soccer?   __No.__ they __don't__.
3. _____ George and Will play football?   _____ they _____.
4. _____ they play hockey?   _____ they _____.

3 *Read the story about Helen and Anna.*

Helen and Anna like sports, too.
They go to a gym.
They lift weights. They swim.
They don't play football. They don't do aerobics.

4 *Write the missing words.*

5. _____ Helen and Anna play football?   _____ they _____.
6. _____ Helen and Anna lift weights?   _____ they _____.
7. _____ they go to a gym?   _____ they _____.
8. _____ they do aerobics?   _____ they _____.

5 *Read the story about Bob and Harriett.*

Bob and Harriett don't work. They are retired.
They exercise often.
They walk. They ride bicycles.
They don't jog. They don't run.

6 *Write the missing words.*

9. _____ Bob and Harriett exercise?   _____ they _____.
10. _____ Bob and Harriett walk?   _____ they _____.
11. _____ they jog?   _____ they _____.
12. _____ they run?   _____ they _____.

26

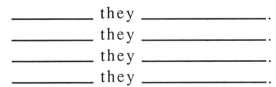 by Paul J. Hamel, © 1990 Delta Systems Co., Inc.

1 Before distributing a copy of the handout, read the story about George and Will to the students as a listening comprehension exercise. Then ask simple "yes/ no" comprehension questions using "do." Example: Question: "Do George and Will like sports?" Have students answer "Yes, they do," or "No, they don't." Distribute the handouts and read the stories again while the students underline unfamiliar vocabulary. Then explain the vocabulary. (You might want to project the story onto a screen or chalkboard using an overhead projector.)

2 Use the fill-in exercises in section 2 as oral drills. (Discourage students from writing. This should be a time for oral practice.) Continue the drill by having students ask original questions using the same structures.

3 Next, have students write in the missing words. (See handwritten examples.) Correct the sentences. You may want to project a copy of the handout that has been transfered to an overhead transparency directly onto a chalkboard where students can write and see the correct answers.

4 Repeat the same procedure for sections 3, 4, 5, and 6.

Follow-Up

• As a class, write a four-line text modeled on the stories on the worksheet about two students in your class. Practice asking and answering questions about the new story.

• Discuss the verbs that are associated with sports:

play hockey	hike	ice skate
play baseball	swim	ski
play basketball	surf	water ski
play football	jog	bowl
play soccer	run	box
play tennis	walk	do aerobics
play volleyball	exercise	do gymnastics
play racquetball	ride bicycles	lift weights
play handball	golf	
play ping-pong	roller skate	

• On a subsequent day, give the stories as a dictation.

Teaching Tip

The following suggestions are only a few of those to be kept in mind when teaching vocabulary.

• Use as many flash cards, objects (realia), and pictures as possible in order to reinforce the words visually. This will help hold interest and aid students in remembering new vocabulary.

• Try eliciting new vocabulary words by means of a sentence in which the last word is not specific. For example, if you want to elicit the word "water," you can say "when I'm thirsty, I drink something. What?" When a student guesses the word, have him or her repeat the original sentence replacing the final word with the specific noun. If nobody can guess the word, say the word and have everybody repeat it in the original sentence. This is a valuable technique because even if the students do not know the word that you are trying to elicit, they are being made aware of the context in which the word in found. It also fosters active listening.

• Define the words and give many contextual examples in sentences, expressions, and situations. Also help define and contrast the new vocabulary with synonyms, antonyms, and homonyms.

• When selecting vocabulary, concentrate on practical, high-frequency, functional vocabulary and expressions.

• Do not overburden your students with too many vocabulary items at any one time. Introduce not more than ten or so new words per lesson.

General   Suggestions

• Create an atmosphere where students are not afraid to make mistakes. Simple communication is more important than speaking perfectly.

• Encourage students to use what they have learned in class in their speech. Encourage them to speak to one another in English during their breaks and free time.

• Be eclectic. Use any method, technique, or combination of methods that work for you and your students.

• Use as much variety in your lessons as possible.

Beginning & Intermediate Levels

14 Filling Out a Form

1 *Directions: Study the registration card and abbreviations.*

"I want to register for a class."

Wanda Perry

REGISTRATION CARD
PRINT FIRMLY

NAME **Perry   Wanda   Marie**
    Last   First   Middle

ADDRESS **8300   Brown St.   Apt. #2**
    Number   Street   Apartment

CITY **Los Angeles** STATE **CA** ZIP CODE **90046**

DATE OF BIRTH **6/28/51** NATIONALITY **Dutch**

CLASS **ESL** LEVEL **3** TELEPHONE **254-4132**

SIGNATURE *Wanda Perry* DATE **10/9/90**

ABBREVIATIONS
St.	=	street
Ave.	=	avenue
Blvd.	=	boulevard
Dr.	=	drive
Rd.	=	road
Apt.	=	apartment
#	=	number
N.	=	north
S.	=	south
E.	=	east
W.	=	west

2 *Fill out the registration card for ROGER BEST.*

REGISTRATION CARD
PRINT FIRMLY

NAME _____
    Last   First   Middle

ADDRESS _____
    Number   Street   Apartment

CITY _____ STATE _____ ZIP CODE _____

DATE OF BIRTH _____ NATIONALITY _____

CLASS _____ LEVEL _____ TELEPHONE _____

SIGNATURE _____ DATE _____

"I'm Roger Best. My middle name is Paul. I want to study English. I'm from Quebec, Canada. I want to be in a level two ESL class. I passed a placement test for level two. I live at 4411 Woodman Ave. La Mesa, California. My zip code is nine-two-zero-four-one. My telephone number is six-one-nine-four-six-nine-three-one-five-seven. I'm twenty-eight years old. My birthday is July second."

Roger Best

3

Please fill out your own registration card.

REGISTRATION CARD
PRINT FIRMLY

NAME _____
    Last   First   Middle

ADDRESS _____
    Number   Street   Apartment

CITY _____ STATE _____ ZIP CODE _____

DATE OF BIRTH _____ NATIONALITY _____

CLASS _____ LEVEL _____ TELEPHONE _____

SIGNATURE _____ DATE _____

BAG OF TRICKS by Paul J. Hamel, © 1990 Delta Systems Co., Inc.

1 Distribute the handout and read the registration card at the top of the page. Make students aware of the street address patterns used in your community. In many English-speaking countries, cities are usually organized in blocks. Each block generally contains one hundred addresses. Odd numbers are used on one side of the street and even numbers on the other side. Some cities, such as Washington, D.C., utilize a grid system dividing the city into N.E., N.W., S.E., and S. W.

On the chalkboard, list the abbreviations along with their nonabbreviated forms. Drill for pronunciation. Allow the students sufficient time to study the list. Then erase the nonabbreviated forms. Divide the class into two teams. Alternately have one member of each team come to the chalkboard. Have the student select a word from the list of abbreviations and write the word beside the corresponding abbreviation. For each correct answer, give one point to the appropriate team. Insist on complete accuracy including spelling and capitalization. You may want to use some of the additional words below.

CA	California	Hwy.	highway	Rm.	room
Cir.	circle	Jr.	junior	Ste.	suite
Co.	county, country	Ln.	lane	TX	Texas
Ct.	court	Pl.	place	NY	New York
D.C.	District of Columbia	P.O.	post office	L. A.	Los Angeles

2 Read the information about Roger Best in the speech balloons. Then, tell the students that they are responsible for filling out the registration card using the information in the speech balloon. Do the first few lines with them. (You may want to project an overhead transparency image directly onto the chalkboard where students can write their answers directly onto the form.)

3 Before having the students fill out the registration card at the bottom of the page, point out the following items that may cause confusion.

1. The meaning of Mr., Mrs., Miss, and Ms.
2. The last name preceding the first name on many forms and applications.
3. The street number preceding the street name.
4. Apartment numbers written as #6, Apt. 6, or Apt. #6 and placed after the street name.
5. Telephone area codes and prefixes.
6. The month as the first element of the date which is expressed either by word or number.

15 Parts of a Car

1 VOCABULARY *Practice the pronunciation of the words.*

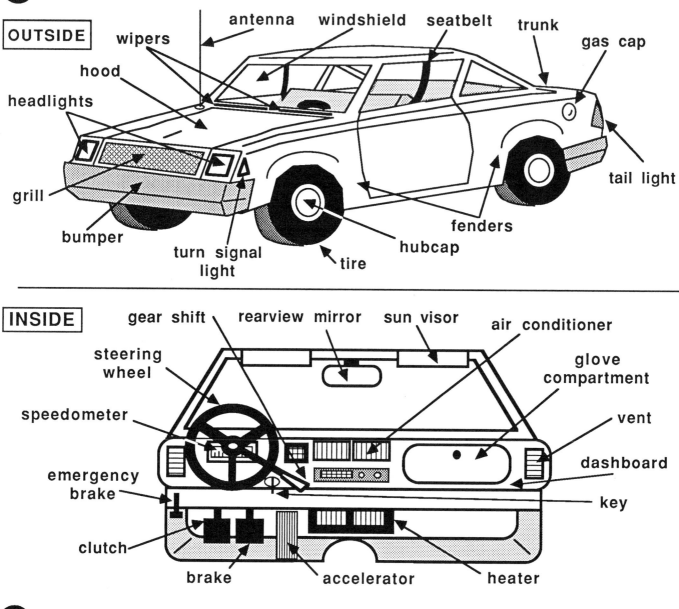

OUTSIDE

antenna windshield seatbelt trunk
wipers
gas cap
hood
headlights
tail light
grill
fenders
hubcap
bumper
turn signal
light
tire

INSIDE

gear shift rearview mirror sun visor air conditioner
steering
wheel
glove
compartment
speedometer
vent
dashboard
emergency
brake
key
clutch
brake accelerator heater

2 PAIR PRACTICE *Talk about the parts of a car. Use the prepositions in the box to describe where they are located.*

on the outside of	on the left side of
on the inside of	in the front of
on the side of	in the back of
on the right side of	at the corner of

Student 1: Where is/are ....?
Student 2: It's/They're ....

1 Read and explain the different parts of the car. Practice the pronunciation of the vocabulary:

OUTSIDE	wipers	trunk	hubcap	grill
	antenna	gas cap	tire	headlights
	windshield	tail light	turn signal light	hood
	seatbelt	fenders	bumper	

INSIDE	gear shift	glove compartment	heater	emergency brake
	rearview mirror	vent	accelerator	speedometer
	sun visor	dashboard	brake	steering wheel
	air conditioner	key	clutch	

2 With the help of a student, demonstrate how to do the pair practice exercise using the pictures and the list of prepositions. Then have the students continue by working in pairs.

3 On the following day, give a short vocabulary quiz using the test below. You may want to project an overhead transparency image directly onto the chalkboard where students can write the answers.

4 As a follow-up exercise, you might want to teach some additional vocabulary:

horn	gas tank	armrest	bucket seats
license plate	headrest	door handle	mat
brake light	door lock	gas gauge	stick shift

VOCABULARY TEST   Name _____ Date _____

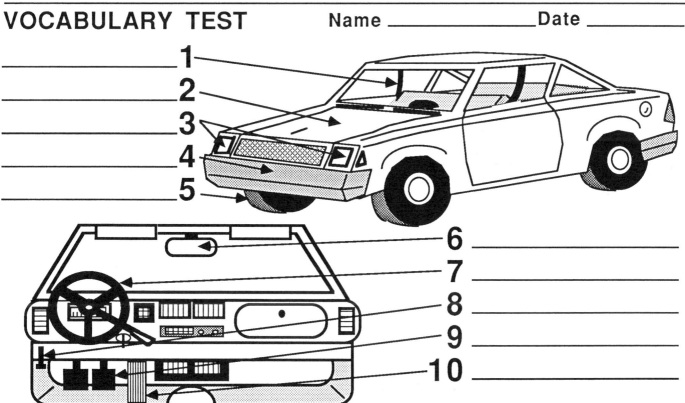

1 _____
2 _____
3 _____
4 _____
5 _____
6 _____
7 _____
8 _____
9 _____
10 _____

16 Weather/Temperature

1 Dictation *Write the missing letters as your teacher reads the words.*

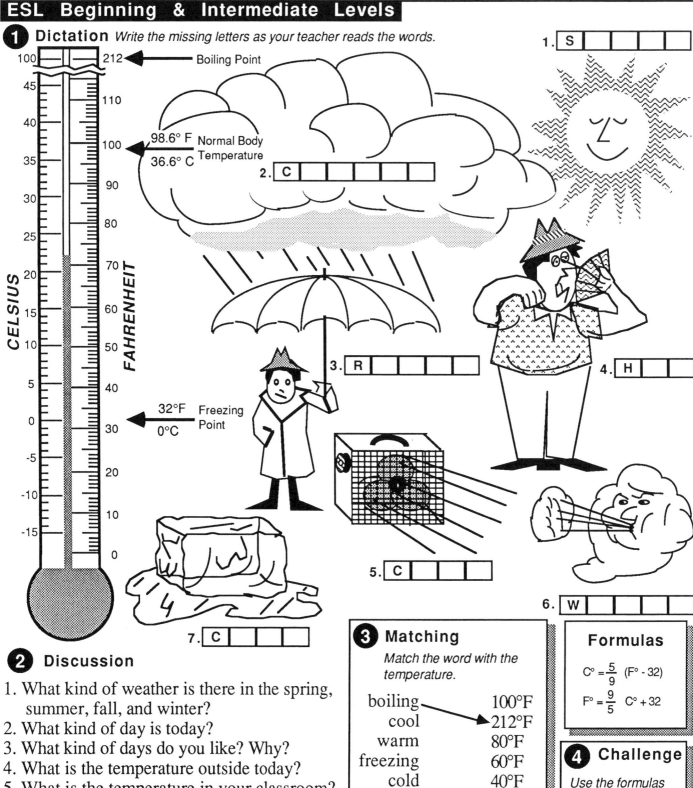

1. S ☐ ☐ ☐ ☐ ☐
2. C ☐ ☐ ☐ ☐ ☐ ☐
3. R ☐ ☐ ☐ ☐ ☐
4. H ☐ ☐ ☐
5. C ☐ ☐ ☐ ☐
6. W ☐ ☐ ☐ ☐ ☐
7. C ☐ ☐ ☐ ☐

2 Discussion

1. What kind of weather is there in the spring, summer, fall, and winter?
2. What kind of day is today?
3. What kind of days do you like? Why?
4. What is the temperature outside today?
5. What is the temperature in your classroom?
6. What is a comfortable room temperature?
7. What is normal body temperature?
8. What is the temperature on the thermometer above?

3 Matching

Match the word with the temperature.

boiling	100°F
cool	212°F
warm	80°F
freezing	60°F
cold	40°F
hot	0°F

Formulas

$$C° = \frac{5}{9} \ (F° - 32)$$

$$F° = \frac{9}{5} \ C° + 32$$

4 Challenge

Use the formulas above to find the equivalent of 20°C.

20°C = _____ °F

1 Before handing out the lesson, introduce key vocabulary. You can do this by eliciting the words by means of a sentence in which the last word is not specific. For example, if you want to elicit the word "water," you can say, "When I'm thirsty, I drink something. What?" When a student guesses the word, have him/her repeat the original sentence replacing the final word with the specific word. If nobody can guess the word, give the word and have everybody repeat the word in the original sentence. This is a valuable technique used in presenting new vocabulary because even if the students do not know the word that you are trying to elicit, they are being aware of the context in which the word is found. Naturally, this cannot be done with very low level classes. In this case, explain the words through pictures, flash card, or by other means, and simply have the students repeat the words after you.

Vocabulary:

sunny	cool	season	winter	wet	storm	Fahrenheit	boiling
cloudy	windy	spring	clear	rain	snow	Centigrade	freezing
rainy	cold	summer	warm	outside	foggy	temperature	formulas
hot	weather	fall/autumn	degree	daytime	smoggy	thermometer	normal
							comfortable

2 Give a dictation as an active listening exercise.

• Dictate the following words, and have students write them on the handout.

1. sunny	3. rainy	5. cool	7. cold
2. cloudy	4. hot	6. windy	

• Correct the dictation. (You may want to project an overhead transparency image directly on to the chalkboard where students can check the answers.)

3 Lead the students in a class discussion based on the questions on the handout.
• Examine the picture of the thermometer at the top of the page.
• Quiz the students by asking questions about the thermometer. Practice finding the equivalent degrees by looking across the thermometer.

4 Using the thermometer, have the students do a pair-practice exercise. Write the rejoinders on the board and do a few examples as practice before having students work in pairs.

Student 1: How much is .... degrees Centigrade?
Student 2: It's about .... degrees Fahrenheit.

5 Have students match the words with the appropriate temperature.

Answers: boiling-212°F, cool-60°F, warm-80°F, freezing-0°F, cold-40°F, hot-100°F.

6 Challenge

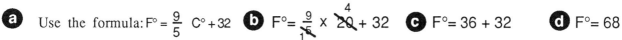 **a** Use the formula: $F° = \frac{9}{5} C° + 32$ **b** $F° = \frac{9}{5} \times \overset{4}{20} + 32$ **c** $F° = 36 + 32$ **d** $F° = 68$

35

17 Safety Signs

1 READ *Sam has some safety signs for his company.*

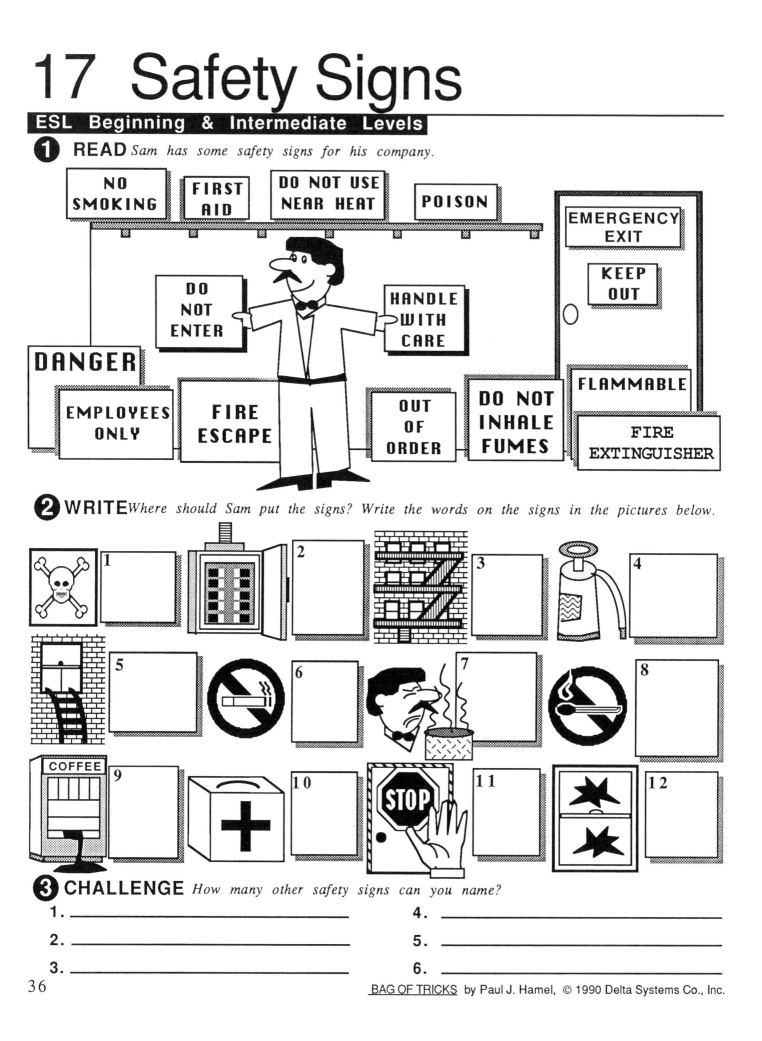

NO SMOKING

FIRST AID

DO NOT USE NEAR HEAT

POISON

EMERGENCY EXIT

KEEP OUT

DO NOT ENTER

HANDLE WITH CARE

DANGER

FLAMMABLE

EMPLOYEES ONLY

FIRE ESCAPE

OUT OF ORDER

DO NOT INHALE FUMES

FIRE EXTINGUISHER

2 WRITE *Where should Sam put the signs? Write the words on the signs in the pictures below.*

3 CHALLENGE *How many other safety signs can you name?*

1. _____
2. _____
3. _____
4. _____
5. _____
6. _____

 BAG OF TRICKS by Paul J. Hamel, © 1990 Delta Systems Co., Inc.

1 Read and explain the meanings of the safety signs in the picture.

Have the students paraphrase the words on the signs as best they can. Examples:

HANDLE WITH CARE	Be careful when you use it.
OUT OF ORDER	It doesn't work.
DO NOT INHALE FUMES	Don't breathe it.
KEEP OUT!	Don't go in.
FLAMMABLE	It can catch fire easily.
POISON	Don't drink it.
DO NOT USE NEAR HEAT	Don't use it where it's hot.
FIRST AID	It's where you can get medical help.

Make two lists on the chalkboard: on the left write the original wording of the sign, and on the right the paraphrased form.

2 Tell the students to write the appropriate safety signs in the boxes next to the pictures in the WRITE exercise on the lower half of the handout.

Answer Key:

1. POISON	5. EMERGENCY EXIT	9. OUT OF ORDER
2. DANGER	6. NO SMOKING	10. FIRST AID
3. FIRE ESCAPE	7. DO NOT INHALE FUMES	11. KEEP OUT
4. FIRE EXTINGUISHER	8. FLAMMABLE	12. DANGER

3 CHALLENGE

• As a homework assignment, have the students make a list of other safety signs. On the following day, make a list of the signs on the chalkboard.

• On a subsequent day, use the list as a dictation exercise.

18 Safety Signs

ESL Beginning & Intermediate Levels

Directions: Fold the page on the dotted line. Look at your side only. Compare your picture after you both fill in all the empty signs.

## Student 1	## Student 2

Fill in the blank signs below with the signs your partner describes and dictates to you.

Describe to your partner the location of the signs in your picture. Read what's on the signs.

FOLD HERE

Now describe to your partner the location of the signs in your picture. Read what's on the signs.

Now fill in the blank signs below with the signs your partner describes and dictates to you.

FOLD HERE

BAG OF TRICKS by Paul J. Hamel, © 1990 Delta Systems Co., Inc.

1 Review some common prepositions:

near   above
next to   below
to the left   under
to the right   over

2 Review the names of the objects on the handout:

cabinet   sign
door   wall
fire extinguisher   water fountain

3 Have students fold the page on the dotted line. Tell them to look at their side of their page only. Explain that the students must fill in the blank signs that their partner describes and dictates. Also, explain that they will have the opportunity to compare pictures after they both finish the exercise.

4 Follow-up Exercise *(for intermediate and advanced students)*

• Dictate the following memo:

INTER-OFFICE MEMO

TO: All Employees

FROM: Safety Coordinator

SUBJECT: SAFETY

There are new safety signs in all work areas and offices. Please read

the signs and do what they say. They are for your safety. There are

also new fire extinguishers. Locate them and remember where they are.

If you see any dangerous situations, please let me know. We want a

safe and healthy work place.

19 Traffic Signs

1 *Fold the page on the dotted line. Look at your side only. Compare your picture after you both fill in all the empty signs.*

2 *Fill in the blank signs below with the signs your partner describes to you.*

2 *Describe to your partner the locations of the signs in your picture. Read what is on them.*

Student 1

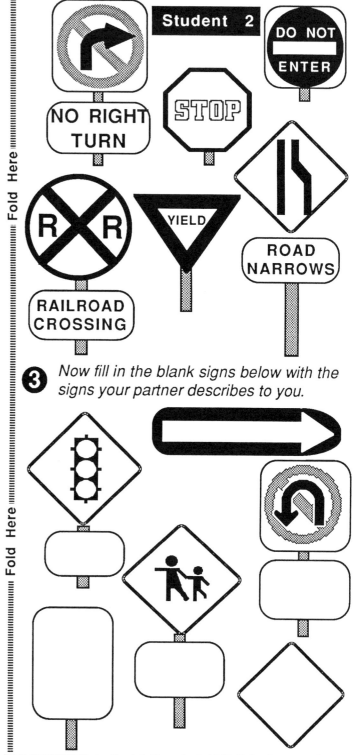

Student 2

3 *Describe to your partner the locations of the signs in your picture. Read what is on them.*

3 *Now fill in the blank signs below with the signs your partner describes to you.*

40

1 Before distributing the handout, review shapes and meanings of the various traffic signs. (You may want to contact your local Department of Motor Vehicles for a driver handbook that contains pictures of all traffic signs.)

octagon	triangle	circle	diamond	square		
stop	yield	railroad crossing	warning	traffic	no passing	school

2 Review the colors and their meanings:

red	=	danger, stop	blue	=	service	
orange	=	construction	white	=	traffic rules	
yellow	=	general warning	brown	=	public recreation areas	
green	=	direction and distance	black	=	night speed limit	

3 On the chalkboard, draw the signs and write their meanings below them. Drill for pronunciation. Then erase the meanings. Divide the class into two teams. Alternately have one member of a team come to the chalkboard. Have him/her select a sign and then write the meaning under it. For each correct answer, give one point to the appropriate team. Insist on complete accuracy.

4 Review prepositions of location using "top", "bottom", "middle", "right", and "left". (i.e., top left, bottom right, middle left, etc.)

5 Distribute the handout. Then have students fold the page on the dotted line. Tell them to look at their side of their page only. Explain that the students must fill in the blank signs that their partner describes and dictates. Also, explain that they will have the opportunity to compare pictures after they both finish the exercise.

6 As a follow-up exercise, you may want to teach the meanings of other signs:

NO STOPPING ANY TIME	RIGHT LANE MUST TURN RIGHT	DIP
TRUCK ROUTE	BUSES AND CAR POOLS ONLY	FLOODED
NO PED CROSSING	GAS FOOD LODGING	SLIDE AREA
NO PARKING ANY TIME	NEXT SERVICES 22 MILES	BUMP
SPEED CHECKED BY RADAR	REST AREA	FALLING ROCKS
NO BICYCLES	SOFT SHOULDER	ROUGH ROAD
DO NOT PASS	PAVEMENT ENDS	LOW CLEARANCE
SLOWER TRAFFIC KEEP RIGHT	NARROW BRIDGE	NOT A THROUGH STREET
TOW AWAY ZONE	TUNNEL	DETOUR AHEAD
EMERGENCY PARKING ONLY	PED XING	OPEN TRENCH
PARK PARALLEL	NO OUTLET	FLAGMAN AHEAD
PASSING LANE AHEAD	SLIPPERY WHEN WET	ROAD WORK AHEAD
BEGIN FREEWAY	THRU TRAFFIC MERGE LEFT	BRIDGE OUT
USE CROSSWALK	ISLANDS	ROAD CLOSED
3-WAY SIGNAL	HILL	PREPARE TO STOP

Teaching Tip

You may want to use the following techniques to develop effective listening comprehensive skills.

• After introducing key vocabulary words that appear in a reading lesson or dialog, slowly read the text aloud to your students before having them look at the written word. Then ask general comprehension questions. As the end of the reading lesson or dialog, read the text again at normal speed. The students should not be allowed to read along; they should concentrate on listening.

• Give frequent short dictations.

• When doing drills or question-and answer exercises, have students cue one another whenever possible. This forces them to listen to each other and become accustomed to different accents.

• Have students work in pairs and groups so that they can listen and respond to one another on a more personal level.

• When practicing dialogs or role-playing, occasionally have pairs of students stand back-to-back so that they must understand each other without the aid of non-verbal (visual) cues.

• Invite a guest speaker, the principal, the school nurse, a police officer, etc., to be interviewed in class so that the students can hear other accents and intonations. Before allowing the students to interview the speaker, prime the class by discussing the kinds of questions they will ask. By practicing the questions beforehand, students will be less embarrassed about asking questions or making mistakes.

• Give students the opportunity to listen to different examples of spoken English through music, games, movies, slide presentations, videos, etc.

Using an Overhead Projector

• Project a copy of the handout that has been transferred to an overhead transparency directly onto a chalkboard where students can write the correct answers to a written exercise.

Intermediate Level

20 Past Tense Regular Verbs

1 *Write the phrases in the boxes as the teacher dictates.*

FEBRUARY

1	2	3	4	5	6	7
8	9	10	11	12	13	14
15	16	17	18	19	20	21
22	23	24	25	26	27	28

2 *Talk with another student. Use the calendar.*

Student 1: What did Sam do on ....?
Student 2: He ....

What did Sam do on February first?

He stayed home.

3 *Use the calendar.*

Student 1: Did he ....?
Student 2: Yes, he did. / No, he didn't.

Did he work on February sixteenth?

No, he didn't.

4 *Talk with another student. Use the phrases below.*

Student 1: When did you last ....?
Student 2: .... ago. What about you?
Student 1: I ....
              or
        I never ....

When did you last work late?

I worked late yesterday.

I worked late last week. What about you?

work late	clean your apartment	watch T.V.	practice English
wash windows	invite people to your home	cook dinner	play tennis
call relatives	call a friend	shop for food	relax

BAG OF TRICKS by Paul J. Hamel, © 1990 Delta Systems Co., Inc.

1. Review the use of the past tense. Explain how to add the "-ed" ending to form the past tense of regular verbs in the affirmative only. We do not use the "-ed" ending with verbs in the question and negative forms. We use "did" with the present tense of a verb to signal the question and "did not" or "didn't" with the present tense of the verb to signal the negative.

2. Before handing out the lesson, practice the phrases below.

3. Hand out the lesson and dictate the phrases. Tell students to write phrases in the boxes.

Feb. 1: stay home
Feb. 2: work late
Feb. 3: mail package
Feb. 4: invite friends to dinner
Feb. 5: answer letters
Feb. 6: move furniture
Feb. 7: clean apartment
Feb. 8: shop for food
Feb. 9: work overtime
Feb.10: attend exercise class

Feb. 11: finish work early
Feb. 12: wash clothes
Feb. 13: cook dinner for friends
Feb. 14: paint living room
Feb. 15: call parents
Feb. 16: no work
Feb. 17: watch T.V. special
Feb. 18: visit library
Feb. 19: open bank account
Feb. 20: help at senior center

Feb. 21: play tennis
Feb. 22: relax at home
Feb. 23: pick up dry cleaning
Feb. 24: exercise
Feb. 25: start work early
Feb. 26: return library books
Feb. 27: fix broken door
Feb. 28: rain, stay home

4. Correct the dictation. (You may want to project an overhead transparency image directly on to the chalkboard where students can check the answers.) Then, have individual students make complete sentences using the phrases. (i.e., "Sam stayed home on February first." or "Sam didn't work on February sixteenth."

5. Using an overhead transparency, practice the pair practice exercises as whole-class oral drills.

6. After the students are familiar with the phrases, have them do the pair practice exercises. Pairing exercises give the students time, especially in large classes, to practice important speaking skills. Have each student choose a partner. (The first few times, you will probably have to go around the classroom and pair up students.) Encourage the students to pair up with different partners each time. While students are doing the exercise, walk around the room, listen to individuals, and correct mistakes.

7. As a follow-up activity, explain the three different ways we pronounce the "-ed" ending.

- When the verb ends in a voiceless sound (except /t/), "-ed" is pronounced /t/.
- When the verb ends in a voiced sound (except /d/), "-ed" is pronounced /d/.
- When the verb ends in a /t/ or /d/ sound, "-ed" is pronounced /id/.

Examples:
"-ed" pronounced /t/: worked, washed, cooked, watched
"-ed" pronounced /d/: opened, closed, cleaned, called
"-ed" pronounced /id/: rested, visited, waited, painted

Dictate the following words randomly. Then, have individuals come up to the chalkboard and write the words in the correct catagory depending on the sound of the final "-ed."

Finally, have students ask and answer questions in the past tense using the words below.

/t/			/d/			/id/		
asked	looked	washed	stayed	closed	listened	decided	rested	visited
danced	practiced	helped	played	opened	lived	ended	started	waited
dressed	thanked	watched	called	learned	loved	needed	painted	wanted
finished	liked	cooked	cleaned	showed	rained			
			returned	arrived	moved			

21 Past Tense Irregular Verbs

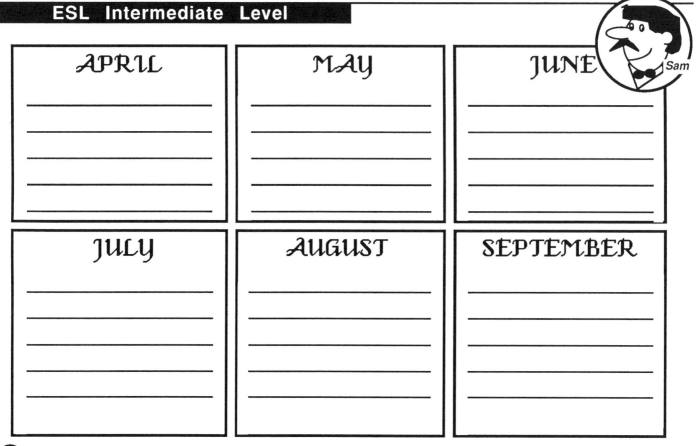

APRIL | MAY | JUNE (Sam)

JULY | AUGUST | SEPTEMBER

1 *Write the phrases in the boxes below the months as the teacher dictates.*

2 *Talk with another student. Use the calendar.*

Student 1: What did Sam do in ....?
Student 2: He ....

What did Sam do in April?

He came to the U.S.

3 *Use the calendar.*

Student 1: Did he ....?
Student 2: Yes, he did. / No, he didn't.

Did he go to work in June?

Yes, he did.

4 *Talk with another student. Use the phrases below.*

Student 1: When did Sam ....?
Student 2: He .... What about you?
Student 1: I ....
    or
    I never ....

When did Sam get a job?

He got a job in June. What about you?

I got a job last March.

get a job	come to this city	have the flu	do your homework
go to work	begin English classes	see a good movie	read a good book
buy a car	take a break	leave home	speak to your family

    BAG OF TRICKS by Paul J. Hamel, © 1990 Delta Systems Co., Inc.

1. Review the use of the past tense. Explain that we use the base form of the verb (infinitive without "to") in the question and negative forms. (Question: Did you go to San Francisco? Negative: No, I didn't go to San Francisco.) We use "did" to signal the question and "didn't" to signal the negative. We use the irregular forms only in the affirmative form.

2. Before handing out the lesson, practice the phrases in the boxes below.

3. Hand out the lesson and dictate the phrases to the students. Tell students to write the phrases under the appropriate month.

April	May	June
• left his country • came to the United States	• went to adult school • took English classes	• found a job • began new job

July	August	September
• met new friend • took driving lessons	• bought a car • had the flu	• got a raise • won the lottery

4. Correct the dictation. (You may want to project an overhead transparency image directly on to the chalkboard where students can check the answers.) Then, have individual students make complete sentences using the phrases. (i.e., "Sam came to the United States in April.)

5. Using an overhead transparency, practice the pair practice exercises as whole-class oral drills.

6. After the students are familiar with the phrases, have them do the pair practice exercises. Pairing exercises give the students time, especially in large classes, to practice important speaking skills. Have each student choose a partner. (The first few times, you will probably have to go around the classroom and pair up students.) Encourage the students to pair up with different partners each time. While students are doing the exercise, walk around the room, listen to individuals, and correct mistakes.

7. Teach other frequently used irregular verbs:

Present	Past	Present	Past	Present	Past
bring	brought	hurt	hurt	sing	sang
choose	chose	keep	kept	sit	sat
cost	cost	know	knew	sleep	slept
do	did	lend	lent	speak	spoke
drink	drank	let	let	spend	spent
drive	drove	lose	lost	spread	spread
eat	ate	make	made	stand	stood
fall	fell	mean	meant	steal	stole
feel	felt	read	read	swim	swam
find	found	ride	rode	teach	taught
fly	flew	run	ran	tell	told
forget	forgot	see	saw	think	thought
give	gave	sell	sold	wake	woke
hear	heard	set	set	wear	wore
hide	hid	shake	shook	write	wrote
hold	held	shut	shut		

22 Apartment Ads

1 *Study the newspaper ads. Then cover the ads in the middle box. Read the ads on the left aloud.*

FURN SING	FURNISHED SINGLE APARTMENT
elev., pkg., A/C	elevator, parking, air conditioning
appl. xlnt cond	appliances, excellent condition
$100. wk.	$100. rent a week
call mgr. eve.	call manager in the evenings
657-8814	657-8814

UNFURN APT	UNFURNISHED APARTMENT
1 bdr + den	one bedroom and a den
C/D, balc.	carpets and drapes, balcony
no pets, $500. mo.	no pets, $500. rent a month
call aft 6 pm	call after 6 p.m.
659-3051	659-3051

UNF. APT	UNFURNISHED APARTMENT
2 + 2	two bedrooms and two bathrooms
2-car gar.	two-car garage
w/fplc., D-wash	with a fireplace, dishwasher
call for appt.	call for an appointment
694-3012	694-3012

CONDO	CONDOMINUM
3bd/2ba	three bedrooms and two bathrooms
nu cpt/drps	new carpets and drapes
pool, sec. bldg	swimming pool, security building
open daily 8-5	open daily from 8 a.m. to 5 p.m.
378-0411	378-0411

UNF. HSE	UNFURNISHED HOUSE
2 bdrm	two bedrooms
frig & stv	refrigerator and stove
lg. bckyd	large backyard
washr/dryr	washer and dryer
call aft 463-1298	call in the afternoon 463-1298

OTHER COMMON ABBREVIATIONS USED IN APARTMENT ADS

bach.	bachelor apartment
beaut.	beautiful
bltins	built-in cabinets
dec.	decorated
dep.	deposit
din. rm.	dining room
fam. rm.	family room
1st/last	first and last month's rent
flrs.	floors
fwy.	freeway
gard.	garden
gd.	good
hdwd. flrs.	hardwood floors
hr.	hour
jac.	jacuzzi
kit.	kitchen
lse.	lease
loc.	location
lux.	luxury
mgr.	manager
nr.	near
own.	owner
pd.	paid
p/p; prvtprty	private party
refs. req.	references required
sep.	separate
twnhse.	townhouse
utils.	utilities
vu.	view
yd.; yrd.	yard

2 *Talk with another student about the ads above.*

Student 1: Does the .... have ....?
Student 2: Yes, it does. / No, it doesn't.

Does the condo have a fireplace?

No, it doesn't.

3 *Write the full words for the abbreviations to the left.*

UNF. APT _____

3 + 2 _____

stv/frig _____

xlnt cond. _____

call mgr. eve. _____

utils. pd. _____

lg. yrd. _____

nu D/C _____

1st mo. dep. _____

A/C _____

BAG OF TRICKS by Paul J. Hamel, © 1990 Delta Systems Co., Inc.

1 Read the ads to the left. Then read the corresponding ads in the middle box. Point out and discuss the abbreviations.

• Tell the students to cover the ads in the middle box. Ask for volunteers to read the ads using only the abbreviations. (You may want to use an overhead projector to project only the abbreviations.)

2 Teach the short dialog. Show how to do this activity with the help of a student. Then have the students continue the exercise by working in pairs or small groups.

Answers

UNF. APT	= Unfurnished apartment
3 + 2	= three bedrooms and two bathrooms
stv/frig	= stove and refrigerator
xlnt cond	= excellent condition
call mgn. eve.	= call the manager in the evening

utils. pd.	= utilities paid
lg. yrd.	= large yard
nu D/C	= new draps and carpets
1st mo. dep.	= first month's deposit
A/C	= air conditioning

3 Read and explain other common abbreviations used in apartment ads in the box at the right of the handout.

4 As a follow-up activity, have the students write an original ad for an apartment on a piece of paper. Put their names on the back of the paper. Then have the students role-play choosing an apartment they would like to rent. The students must discuss the rental arrangements with the author of the ad, who acts as the owner of the apartment.

5 For more advanced students, you may want to teach additional vocabulary:

appliances	garden	smoke detector
attic	heater	stairs
basement	laundry room	trash bin
chandelier	patio	Venetian blinds
closet	radiator	wet bar
fence	security locks	
fireplace	shades	

49

23 Filling Out Checks

1 *Study the example of a personal check.*

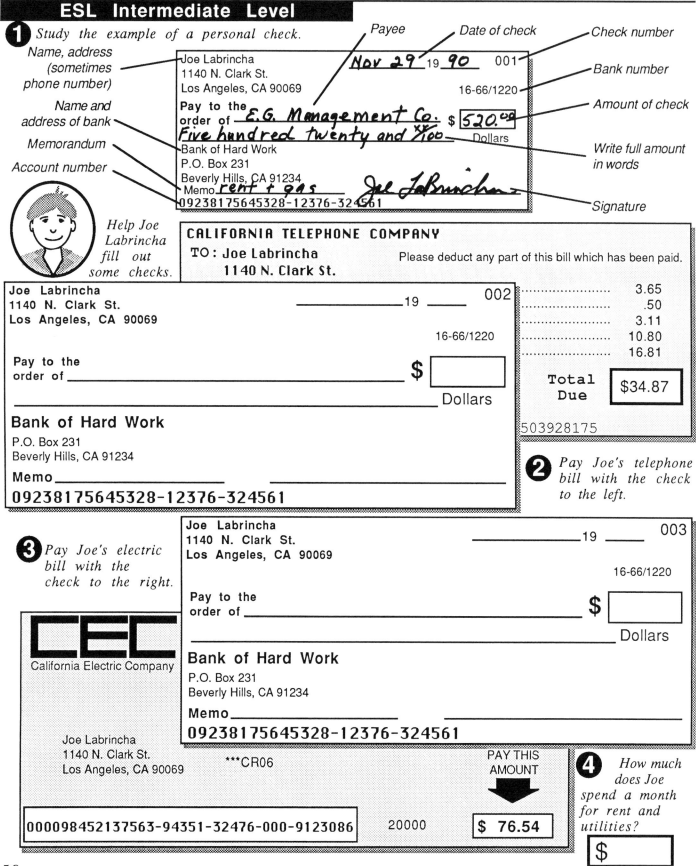

Name, address (sometimes phone number)

Name and address of bank

Memorandum

Account number

Payee

Date of check

Check number

Bank number

Amount of check

Write full amount in words

Signature

Joe Labrincha
1140 N. Clark St.
Los Angeles, CA 90069

Nov 29 19 90   001

16-66/1220

Pay to the order of   E.G. Management Co. $ 520.00
Five hundred twenty and XX/100 — Dollars

Bank of Hard Work
P.O. Box 231
Beverly Hills, CA 91234
Memo rent + gas   Joe Labrincha
09238175645328-12376-324561

Help Joe Labrincha fill out some checks.

CALIFORNIA TELEPHONE COMPANY

TO : Joe Labrincha
1140 N. Clark St.

Please deduct any part of this bill which has been paid.

	3.65
	.50
	3.11
	10.80
	16.81
Total Due	$34.87

503928175

2 *Pay Joe's telephone bill with the check to the left.*

Joe Labrincha
1140 N. Clark St.
Los Angeles, CA 90069

_____ 19 ____   002

16-66/1220

Pay to the order of _____ $ _____

_____ Dollars

Bank of Hard Work

P.O. Box 231
Beverly Hills, CA 91234

Memo _____ _____

09238175645328-12376-324561

3 *Pay Joe's electric bill with the check to the right.*

Joe Labrincha
1140 N. Clark St.
Los Angeles, CA 90069

_____ 19 ____   003

16-66/1220

Pay to the order of _____ $ _____

_____ Dollars

Bank of Hard Work

P.O. Box 231
Beverly Hills, CA 91234

Memo _____ _____

09238175645328-12376-324561

CEC
California Electric Company

Joe Labrincha
1140 N. Clark St.
Los Angeles, CA 90069

***CR06

PAY THIS AMOUNT

000098452137563-94351-32476-000-9123086   20000 $ 76.54

4 *How much does Joe spend a month for rent and utilities?*

$ _____

Review the new vocabulary:

pay to the order of	signature	rent
memorandum	deduct	gas
account number	bill	utilities
payee	check	full amount

Project a copy of the handout on an overhead transparency directly onto the chalkboard where the students can later fill out the checks.

2 Explain how to read the telephone and electric bill. Then, have students fill out the blank checks. Check answers by having individuals fill in the checks onto the projected image on the chalkboard.

3 Have students calculate how much Joe Labrincha pays monthly for rent and utilities and compare it with what the students in your class pay:

Rent and gas:	$520.00
Telephone:	34.87
Electricity:	76.54
TOTAL:	$631.41

4 As a follow-up exercise, bring some department store catalogs or newspaper ads and some blank checks. (If you do not have any blank checks, you may want to photo copy the check below.) Tell the students that they have a a certain budget to buy the necessary items to set up a household. Have the students purchase each item by writing out a separate check. Also, have them keep a running balance. Discuss and make a list of what your students decided were necessary items to set up a household.

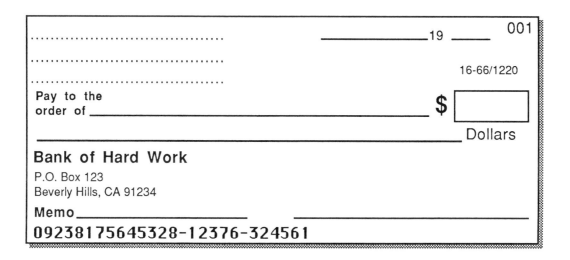

24 Height and Weight

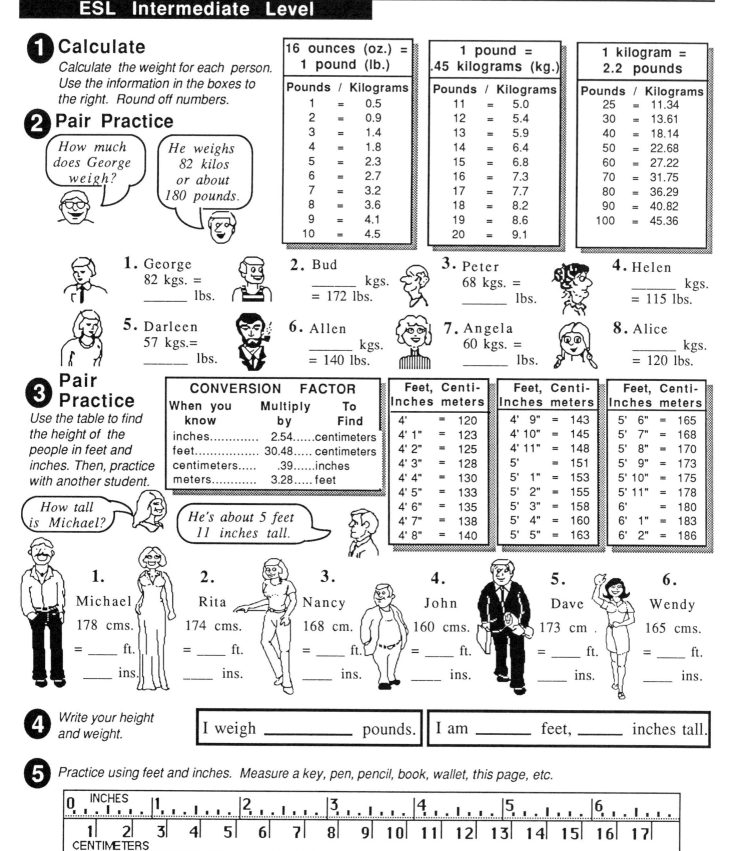

1 Calculate

Calculate the weight for each person. Use the information in the boxes to the right. Round off numbers.

16 ounces (oz.) = 1 pound (lb.)	
Pounds	Kilograms
1 =	0.5
2 =	0.9
3 =	1.4
4 =	1.8
5 =	2.3
6 =	2.7
7 =	3.2
8 =	3.6
9 =	4.1
10 =	4.5

1 pound = .45 kilograms (kg.)	
Pounds	Kilograms
11 =	5.0
12 =	5.4
13 =	5.9
14 =	6.4
15 =	6.8
16 =	7.3
17 =	7.7
18 =	8.2
19 =	8.6
20 =	9.1

1 kilogram = 2.2 pounds	
Pounds	Kilograms
25 =	11.34
30 =	13.61
40 =	18.14
50 =	22.68
60 =	27.22
70 =	31.75
80 =	36.29
90 =	40.82
100 =	45.36

2 Pair Practice

How much does George weigh?

He weighs 82 kilos or about 180 pounds.

1. George 82 kgs. = _____ lbs.

2. Bud _____ kgs. = 172 lbs.

3. Peter 68 kgs. = _____ lbs.

4. Helen _____ kgs. = 115 lbs.

5. Darleen 57 kgs.= _____ lbs.

6. Allen _____ kgs. = 140 lbs.

7. Angela 60 kgs. = _____ lbs.

8. Alice _____ kgs. = 120 lbs.

3 Pair Practice

Use the table to find the height of the people in feet and inches. Then, practice with another student.

CONVERSION FACTOR		
When you know	Multiply by	To Find
inches............	2.54......	centimeters
feet................	30.48.....	centimeters
centimeters.....	.39......	inches
meters...........	3.28.....	feet

Feet, Inches	Centimeters
4' =	120
4' 1" =	123
4' 2" =	125
4' 3" =	128
4' 4" =	130
4' 5" =	133
4' 6" =	135
4' 7" =	138
4' 8" =	140

Feet, Inches	Centimeters
4' 9" =	143
4' 10" =	145
4' 11" =	148
5' =	151
5' 1" =	153
5' 2" =	155
5' 3" =	158
5' 4" =	160
5' 5" =	163

Feet, Inches	Centimeters
5' 6" =	165
5' 7" =	168
5' 8" =	170
5' 9" =	173
5' 10" =	175
5' 11" =	178
6' =	180
6' 1" =	183
6' 2" =	186

How tall is Michael?

He's about 5 feet 11 inches tall.

1. Michael 178 cms. = ____ ft. ____ ins.

2. Rita 174 cms. = ____ ft. ____ ins.

3. Nancy 168 cm. = ____ ft. ____ ins.

4. John 160 cms. = ____ ft. ____ ins.

5. Dave 173 cm. = ____ ft. ____ ins.

6. Wendy 165 cms. = ____ ft. ____ ins.

4 Write your height and weight.

I weigh _____ pounds.

I am _____ feet, _____ inches tall.

5 Practice using feet and inches. Measure a key, pen, pencil, book, wallet, this page, etc.

INCHES 0 1 2 3 4 5 6

CENTIMETERS 1 2 3 4 5 6 7 8 9 10 11 12 13 14 15 16 17

Using Feet, Inches, & Pounds

1 Read and discuss the information on weight at the top of the page. Practice the structure " . . . pounds equals . . . point . . . kilos (kilograms)." Use the word "point" for the decimal point. Examples: "One pound equals point five kilos" and "Three pounds equal one point four kilos." Also, point out abbreviations. Then ask basic comprehension questions as the following: "How many pounds are there in one kilo?" and "How many kilos are there in three pounds?"

2 Read the names and weights of the people. Then, have students calculate the people's weight in kilograms and pounds. Use the table or formulas (1 lb. = .45 kgs. or 1 kg. = 2.2 lbs.). Be sure to round off numbers.

• Read and practice the question and answer in the speech balloons: "How much does George weigh?" and "He weighs 82 kilos or about 180 pound." Continue the drill substituting the weights. Finally, pair students and have them practice the drill again orally.

• Correct the sentences. You may want to project a copy of the handout that has been transferred to an overhead transparency directly onto a chalkboard where students can write the correct answers.

Answers
1. 82 kgs. = 180 lbs.   4. 52 kgs. = 115 lbs.   7. 60 kgs. = 132 lbs.
2. 78 kgs. = 172 lbs.   5. 57 kgs. = 125 lbs.   8. 55 kgs. = 120 lbs.
3. 68 kgs. = 150 lbs.   6. 64 kgs. = 140 lbs.

3 Use the same methodology for teaching the use of feet/inches described above.

Answers
1. 178 cms. = 5' 11"   3. 168 cms. = 5' 7"   5. 173 cms. = 5' 9"
2. 174 cms. = 5' 9 1/2"   4. 160 cms. = 5' 4"   6. 165 cms. = 5' 6"

4 Discuss desired height and weight. See tables below. Vocabulary: "overweight," "average," or "underweight."

Men*			
Height	Weight	Height	Weight
5' 3"	130 - 153	5' 11"	146 - 184
5' 5"	134 - 160	6' 1"	152 - 192
5' 7"	138 - 168	6' 3"	158 - 202
5' 9"	142 - 176		

Women			
Height	Weight	Height	Weight
4' 11"	103 - 134	5' 7"	123 - 163
5' 1"	106 - 140	5' 9"	129 - 170
5' 3"	111 - 144	5' 11"	135 - 176
5' 5"	117 - 155		

5 Have students find their own weight and height. Have them write the information in the spaces provided.

6 Practice using the ruler at the bottom of the page. Measure small items such as keys, pens, pencils, books, wallets, etc.

* Specialist's Pocket Reference © 1990, Travcom, Inc.

Teaching Tip

Do not underestimate the usefulness of dictation. It can be a very effective tool for practicing the four language skills (listening, speaking, reading, writing). It is especially useful as a warm-up exercise at the beginning of the class period to review previously covered materials. Frequent short dictations focusing on commonly used words and expressions used in simple sentences, and stressing function words, such as articles, prepositions, pronouns, and auxilary verbs, will do much to improve students' writing and spelling. Once students become accustomed to the simple dictation, you may want to vary the dictation format to keep interest high. As an example, try the following:

• Dictate six questions.

• After the students have written six questions in their notebooks, ask six volunteers to write the questions on the chalkboard.

• Have six other students read and correct the questions.

• Have six more volunteers go up to the chalkboard and write the answers to the questions.

• Have students read and correct the answers.

• Discuss additional possible answers to the questions.

Other Suggestions

• Dictate the answers, and then have students write the questions.

• Dictate single words that students must use in complete sentences.

• Dictate jumbled sentences that students must put into the correct word order.

• Dictate short cloze (where every sixth word or so is missing) passages. Then have students try to guess the missing words.

Intermediate & Advanced Levels

25 Using a Library

ESL Intermediate & Advanced Levels

Directions: Find and write the answers to the questions below. Also write the name of the source you used and and the page on which the information was found. There are 100 possible points.

1. Who was the 16th president of the United States? **10** points

_____

Source: _____

Page: _____

2. How is the word "psyche" pronounced? **5** points

_____

Source: _____

Page: _____

3. Does your library use the Dewey Decimal or the Library of Congress classification system? **15** points

_____

Source: _____

4. What is the population of your city or town? **5** points

_____

Source: _____

Page: _____

5. When did Hawaii become a state? **10** points

_____
(date and year)

Source: _____

Page: _____

6. What is the telephone number of the local adult school? **5** points

_____

Source: _____

Page: _____

7. What time will sunrise and sunset be tomorrow? **10** points

Sunrise:_____ a.m.
Sunset:_____ p.m.

Source: _____

Page: _____

8. What is the time difference between Tokyo, Japan and your city? **10** points

_____ *hours*

Source: _____

Page: _____

9. What is an oenophile? **5** points

_____

_____

Source: _____

Page: _____

10. What states border Wyoming? **10** points

_____ _____
_____ _____
_____ _____

Source: _____

Page: _____

11. How many volumes does the largest encyclopedia in the library have? **5** points

_____

Source: _____

Page: _____

12. How many job ads are there for teachers in the newspaper? **10** points

_____ *job ads*

Source: _____

Page: _____

Total Points: [   ]

BAG OF TRICKS by Paul J. Hamel, © 1990 Delta Systems Co., Inc.

❶ Introduction

The objective of this activity is to allow students to visit, use, and explore a library. This exercise uses a scavenger hunt type of game as a learning tool.

Contact the school or city librarian and arrange a time for your class to visit the library, preferably when no other students are there. If no library is available you may want to bring some reference materials into the classroom: an encyclopedia, an atlas, a dictionary, a newspaper, a telephone book, a thesaurus, and an almanac. While it is possible to do the exercise this way, it is not recommended.

❷ The Activity

• While in the library, hand out the worksheet and read the directions and all the questions making sure that the students completely understand all the vocabulary and know what to do.

• Show the location of the reference materials, the card catalog, magazine and newspaper section, reference area, etc.

• Tell the students that they have 45 minutes to find all the information and write their answers on the worksheet.

• Explain that the person or team who gets the most points will win a prize (e. g., a book, a dictionary, or even a piece of candy). If there is limited time, consider allowing students to work in teams. In case of a tie, flip a coin or choose the neatest paper to determine the winner. The teacher should act as a consultant who may give clues, but no answers. The teacher should also help direct students to the correct resources.

• After the time is up, assemble the class, have students exchange papers, and correct the exercise.

• Applaud the winner and present the prize.

Answers:

1. Abraham Lincoln
2. SI-Kee
3. Answers will vary
4. Answers will vary
5. August 21, 1959
6. Answers will vary
7. Answers will vary
8. Answers will vary
9. A connoisseur of wine
10. Montana, South Dakota, Nebraska, Colorado, Utah, and Idaho
11. Answers will vary
12. Answers will vary

❸ Follow-up Activities

• Hand out blank index cards.

• Ask students to write a question on one side of a white index card and write the answer and the source in which it was found on the back of the card. Have the students write their names on the card.

• Collect the cards and use them as the basis of a game. Divide the class into two teams. Teams take turns answering the questions and telling where the information can be found. If a student is asked his or her own question, pass to the next question. If the answer is correct, the team collects a point. The team with the most points wins.

26 Telling a Story

Directions: Fill in the correct form of the past tense, then write a beginning to the story.

A Small Piece of Glass

_____

_____

_____

_____

_____

_____

Eric **walked** up the ramp into the space craft. He _____ he should not have
walk   know
gone. His curiosity had gotten him into trouble before, but this time it _____ more than
                                                                                  be
curiosity; there _____ some kind of force pulling him through the door.   Inside, he
                   be
_____ a strange presence; he _____ that he _____ in a large room. He _____
feel   sense   be   see
wonderfully unfamiliar colors dancing on the walls and _____ faint musical notes.   On
                                                          hear
the floor next to him, there _____ some small shiny objects that _____ out a
                               be   give
weak light.   He _____ down to pick one up, and a human-like figure _____.
                  bend   appear
Eric _____ still; he _____ not move because a strange force _____
       stand   can   have
control.   The figure _____ out a hand full of the small pieces of glass, and the boy
                        hold
_____ one. Nervously, Eric _____, "Who are you?' The figure _____ nothing.
take   ask   say
Suddenly the doors of the space craft _____ , and Eric _____ to the floor as the
                                         shut   fall
craft _____ and _____ upwards into the sky. He _____ that he would
        shake   move   think
never see his family, friends, or even the Earth again. He _____ to feel panic.
                                                            begin
The figure _____ closer, _____ to a door, and _____ Eric to follow. As
             come   point   signal
they _____ the door, Eric _____ a loud knock. The door _____ and Eric
       approach   hear   open
_____ a familiar voice.   "Wake up! It's time to get up! Breakfast will be ready in five
recognize
minutes," his mother _____. Eric _____ his eyes, _____ up in bed and
                       say   open   sit
_____ to smile. Getting out of bed, he _____ back the blankets and _____
begin   pull   hear
something fall to the floor. He _____ up a small piece of glass, _____ his head,
                                  pick   scratch
and _____ where it had come from.
      wonder

   BAG OF TRICKS by Paul J. Hamel, © 1990 Delta Systems Co., Inc

❶ Introduction

- Discuss the following questions. Use the past tense.
1. What was the last science fiction movie that you saw? Describe it.
2. Do you believe that there is intelligent life in outer space?
3. Have you ever seen or known someone who has seen an unidentified flying object (UFO)?
4. What would you do if you saw a UFO or alien from another planet?
5. How do you think the world would greet visitors from another planet?

❷ Language Activities

- Review the use of the regular and irregular verbs in the past tense. You may want to drill the verbs with flash cards by writing the present tense on one side and the past tense on the reverse side. To drill the question and negative forms of irregular verbs, show the students the side of the card containing the past tense, then ask them to ask questions using question words (what, where, when, why, how, etc.). The students will be forced to change the verb form and will have to use the word on the reverse side of the card. Ask another student to answer the question. Show the appropriate word for the affirmative or negative answer.

- Introduce the new vocabulary.

ramp	faint (adj.)	spacecraft	to approach
curiosity	human-like figure	Earth	to scratch
presence	escape	panic	to wonder

- Before handing out a copy of the story, read it to the students as a listening comprehension exercise. Then ask simple comprehension questions.

- Hand out the worksheet and read the story again. Discuss any unfamiliar words.

- Ask the students to change the verbs to the past tense. (You may want to project a copy of the story that has been put on an overhead transparency directly onto the chalkboard, where students can write the correct answers.)

- Discuss several possible beginnings to the story with the students, then ask them to write a beginning to the story.

❸ Follow-up Activities

- Discuss the significance of the piece of glass.
- Have students write an ending to the story.

27 Inviting a Speaker

ESL Intermediate & Advanced Levels

Directions: Write a short article describing the interview. Use strong verbs.

School News

Special Edition

farming he
stunted by
g the rows
the century
t 30 years
eather ser-
ntinues, it
record, not
ven half as
ds of other
e potential
abnormally
cussed the
the key to
ves a tract
ick-hard."
dred of tho
rd E. Lyng
frying sun
eeks, ago, a
logized for
verning el-
rst specific
they repre-
because of
. will raise
ld, in part,
red indus-
; European
rst specific
s failing to
es to push
of the city
he past and
on't have a
faired well
to get him
rather than
much as he
't have the
n the city's
a coalition
city well.
ll the need

Title ______________________________

By *(your name)* ____________________

School News Staff Writer

____________ — ______________________________

(Place)

____

____

____

____

____

____

____

____

____

____

____

____

____

____

____

____

____

UC

Los Angele
Now is the
of well wis
Still, Ripst
sometimes
given way t
some time
myself sor
days at wor
to be with
married las
have the pl

Respresenta
the rapidly
environmen
forth terms,
Bradley is g
consults an
a group and
articulates a
ment that he
further ens
Westside cc
Latinos on t
But as he
tions in city
fice and is
these offica
basis but ra
as consensu
and commu
affluent grc
appointment
certain City
examination
a likeable p
talent for q

❶ Introduction

• Invite a person from your community or school to be interviewed by your class. If there is no one available from the community, consider inviting someone from your school: the principal, assistant principal, counselor, school nurse, security person, clerk, plant manager, or custodian. A few days before the actual visit, prime the class by discussing the topics the students would like to talk about with the guest.

• Discuss and practice the use of the following words when used in direct speech.

Mr.	*Miss.*	*Dr.*	*Ma'am*	*Officer*	*Your Majesty*
Mrs.	*Ms.*	*Sir*	*Your Honor*	*Mr. President*	*Your Holiness*

• Tell the students that they will be responsible for taking notes during the interview and for writing a short article describing what the guest said.

❷ Language Activities

• Review the use of the verbs "say" and "tell." Note the difference in their usage:
A person "says something to somebody." A person "tells somebody something."

2. Expand the exercise by practicing the use of strong verbs to replace "say" and "tell":

state	*report*	*describe*	*express*	*notify*
respond	*answer*	*speculate*	*inform*	*reply*
explain	*illustrate*	*propose*	*announce*	*remark*

• Explain the structure of indirect speech in the affirmative, imperative, and interrogative.

Affirmative	Imperative	Interrogative
Pronouns must change to agree with the new sentence, and the usual sequence of tense must be followed. Example: **Direct** *John said, "I'm hungry."* **Indirect** *John said he was hungry.*	Use the infinitive to express a command. Example: **Direct** *Mary told me, "Go home."* **Indirect** *Mary told me to go home.*	Express the original question in statement form. Example: **Direct** *Mary asked, "Where does John work?"* **Indirect** *Mary asked where John worked.* Introduce a question with "if" or "whether" if the sentence does NOT begin with a question word. Example: **Direct** *Mary asked, "Does John work here?"* **Indirect** *Mary asked if John worked here.*

• Discuss polite ways to ask questions:
Could you please tell us ... ?   *Would you please ... ?*
Please tell us ...   *What do you think about ... ?*

• Conduct the interview. (45 minutes to 1 hour)

• After the guest leaves, discuss what was said in the interview.

• Hand out the work sheet and ask the students to write a short article describing the interview. Also ask them to use some of the strong verbs in #2 above. After correcting the stories, ask volunteers to share their stories.

• Have the students write thank you notes to the guest.

28 Reading Job Ads

1 Study the newspaper ads. Then cover the ads in the middle box.
Read the ads on the left aloud.

CASHIER	CASHIER
p.t./f.t.	part time or full time
loc. exp. des.	local experience desirable
Apply in person,	Apply in person,
XYZ Co.	XYZ Company
321 Main St.	321 Main Street

CARPENTER	CARPENTER
xlnt. bene.	excellent benefits
pd. med./den. ins.	paid medical and dental insurance
Call Mr. Wood	Call Mister Wood
for appt.	for an appointment
657-8814	657-8814

CONSTRUCTION	CONSTRUCTION
gd. work cond.	good working conditions
pd. hol. & vac.	paid holidays and vacations
Send res. to	Send resume
Miss Booker	Miss Booker
1133 Clark Street	1133 Clark Street

AUTO MECH.	AUTO MECHANIC
min. 2 yrs. exp.	minimum two years experience
hi. sal.	high salary
Tel. Apex Motors,	Telephone Apex Motors
993-4363	993-4363
for int.	for an interview

SALESPERSON	SALESPERSON
ref. req.	references required
no. exp. nec.	no experience necessary
Contact Hitec Corp.	Contact Hitec Corporation
P. O. Box 105	Post Office Box 105
Centerville, CA	Centerville, California

OTHER COMMON ABBREVIATIONS USED IN JOB ADS

ad.	advertisement
appoint.	appointment
appl.	application
ASAP	as soon as possible
avail.	available
bkgrnd.	background
bus.	business
cond.	condition
ctr.	center
dept.	department
dntn.	downtown
dr. lic.	driver's license
ed.	education
equip.	equipment
etc.	et cetera
ext.	extension
eve.	evenings
gen.	general
hr.	hour
immed.	immediate
info.	information
max.	maximum
m/f	male or female
off.	office
OT	overtime
perm.	permanent
pri.	private
pref.	preferred
supv.	supervisor
trans.	transporation
vac.	vacation.

SYMBOLS

@	at, each
#	number
$	dollar
%	percent
&	and
-	minus
+	plus
=	equal
/	or
5'	5 feet
9"	9 inches

2 Talk with another student about the ads above.

Student 1: What does .... mean?
Student 2: It means ....

> What does "p.t." mean?

> It means "part time."

3 Write the full words for the abbreviations to the left.

Call for int.	*Call for interview*
xlnt. work cond.	_____
gd. sal.	_____
exp. req.	_____
loc. exp.	_____

Tel. for app.	_____
p.t./f.t.	_____
pd. vac.	_____
med. pd.	_____
ref. nec.	_____

 BAG OF TRICKS by Paul J. Hamel, © 1990 Delta Systems Co., Inc.

1 Read the ads to the left. Then read the corresponding ads in the middle box. Point out and discuss the abbreviations.

Tell the students to cover the ads in the middle box. Ask for volunteers to read the ads using only the abbreviations. (You may want to use an overhead projector to project only the abbreviations.)

2 Teach the short dialog. Show how to do this activity with the help of a student. Then have the students continue the exercise by working in pairs or small groups.

Answers:

Call for int.	= Call for an interview
xlnt. work cond.	= excellent working conditions
gd. sal.	= good salary
exp. req.	= experience required
loc. exp.	= local experience

Tel. for app.	= Telephone for application
p.t./f.t.	= part time or full time
pd. vac.	= paid vacation
med. in. pd.	= medical insurance paid
ref. nec.	= references necessary

3 Read and explain other common abbreviations and symbols used in job ads in the box at the right of the handout.

4 As a follow-up activity, have the students write an original ad for a job on a piece of paper. Put their names on the back of the paper. Then have the students role-play interviewing for the ad. The students must discuss the requirements with the author of the ad, who acts as the interviewer.

6 For more advanced students, you may want to discuss the following topics:
* How should a person dress for an interview?
* What kind of questions are asked during an interview?
* How can a person prepare for an interview?
* What are some places to look for a job?
* What are some do's and don'ts during an interview?
* What are some differences in employment between this country and other countries?
* What kind of information should a person include in a resume?
* In your opinion, what is an acceptable hourly wage?

29 Job Application

APPLICATION FOR EMPLOYMENT
Please print

NAME _____ DATE _____
            Last   *First*   *Middle*   *Month*   *Date*   *Year*

ADDRESS _____
         Number   *Street*   *Apartment Number*   *City*   *State*   *Zip Code*

TELEPHONE Home ( ) _____ Work ( ) _____
                  Area Code   *Area Code*

PLACE OF BIRTH _____
               City   *Country*

CITIZEN OF WHAT COUNTRY? _____

IN CASE OF ACCIDENT CALL _____
                           Name   *Telephone*   *Relationship*

    Address _____
            Number   *Street*   *City*

EDUCATION	NAME AND LOCATION	DATES	COURSE OF STUDY	DEGREE
Elementary School				
High School				
Adult School or Job Training Program				
College or University				

WORK EXPERIENCE
List most recent employment first

COMPANY	LOCATION	DATES	POSITION	REASON FOR LEAVING
		from____to____		
		from____to____		
		from____to____		
		from____to____		

Signature _____

1 Before having the students fill out the application, point out the following items that may cause confusion:

- The meaning of Mr., Mrs., Miss, and Ms.
- The last name preceding the first name on many forms and applications
- The street number preceding the street name
- Apartment numbers written as #6, Apt. 6, or Apt. #6 and placed after the street name
- Telephone area codes and prefixes
- The month as the first element of the date which is expressed either by word or number. Caution students not to use Roman numerals.
- Illegal questions: In the United States, it is against the law to ask certain questions on employment applications (i.e., race, religion, sex, and age).

2 Make an overhead transparency of the application and project it onto the chalkboard. Fill out the application on the chalkboard as a whole-class exercise. Ask a student to volunteer the information asked in the application.

3 Distribute application forms and ask the students to fill them out. Tell them to use the application on the chalkboard as a model. Explain that the form is a convenient information sheet to take along when applying for a job in person. Encourage the students to fold the form and place it in their wallets.

4 Follow-Up Activities

1. Many applications require applicants to respond to written directions such as "check, underline, print, circle, cross out," etc. Practice using these words in the exercise below. Have the students take a piece of paper. Dictate each instruction below. Then demonstrate each appropriate action on the chalkboard.

- On line one, print your name.
- On the second line, write numbers 1 to 10.
- Underline your last name.
- Circle your first name.
- Check the first line.

- Cross out number 6.
- Underline number 9.
- Circle number 1.
- Cross out number 10.
- Check the second line.

2. Have advanced students role-play job interviews in front of the class. (Use volunteers.) One student is the employer and the second is an applicant. Use some of the items on the application. The rest of the class rates the interview with the rating form below.

	Very Good	Good	Fair	Poor	Bad
Posture					
Manners					
Language					
Voice					
Eye Contact					
Attitude					
Personality					
Self-Confidence					
Personal Appearance					

30 Driving Test

Fill in the spaces below with the words in the box. Use the map.

ONE WAY	right
YIELD	25
left	Second and A
stopped	railroad crossing
turned	DO NOT ENTER

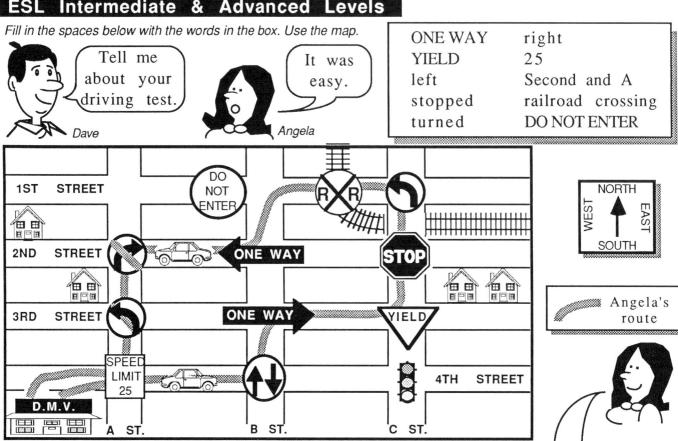

I passed my driving test. I did very well. Let me tell you all about it. We began at the Department of Motor Vehicles at the corner of 4th and A Streets. The sign at the corner said that the speed limit was (1) __25__ miles per hour. I drove east to 4th and B Streets and turned (2) _____. I went one block and turned (3) _____ on 3rd Street. I drove one block. I saw a sign at the corner of 3rd and C Streets. It said (4) _____, so I drove slowly. Then, I (5) _____ north. I (6) _____ at the corner of 2nd and C Streets. After I turned west, I crossed a (7) _____ _____. I drove to 1st and B Streets. I saw a sign there. It said (8) ____ _____ _____, so I didn't continue on 1st Street. I turned south, went one block and turned west on 2nd Street because it's a (9) _____ _____ street. I drove one block, and then turned south at (10) _____ _____ _____ Streets. I drove past 3rd Street and arrived back at the Department of Motor Vehicles.

 BAG OF TRICKS by Paul J. Hamel, © 1990 Delta Systems Co., Inc.

1 Review the meanings of the traffic signs in the map at the top of the handout. (You may want to contact your local Department of Motor Vehicles for driver handbook that contains pictures of all traffic signs.)

2 Explain how to fill in the words in the fill-in exercise. Read the words in the box at the top of the page, read the directions, and do a few examples with the whole class. Correct the exercise by having volunteers read parts of the text aloud.

Answers

1. 25	5. turned	9. one way
2. left	6. stopped	10. Second and A
3. right	7. railroad crossing	
4. yield	8. do not enter	

3 Have students change the story from the past to the imperative. Example:

- Begin at the Department of Motor Vehicles at the corner of 4th and A Streets.
- Drive east to 4th and B Streets and turn left.
- Go one block and turn right on 3rd Street.
- Drive one block.
- Turn north.
- Stop at the corner of 2nd and C Streets, then go to 1st and C Streets.
- After you turn west, cross a railroad crossing.
- Drive to 1st and B Streets.
- Turn south, go one block, and turn west on 2nd Street.
- Drive one block, and then turn south at 2nd and A Streets.
- Drive past 3rd Street and arrive back at the Department of Motor Vehicles.

4 Practice giving directions by having students explain how to go from school to various places in your community.

5 For additional practice, try arranging desks, tables, and chairs as an obstacle course. Have one students direct a blind-folded student through the course by giving oral directions.

6 As a follow-up activity, have the students bring in a map of the city, Ask them to find government buildings, fire department, hospital, schools, religious institutions, airports, bus stations, cultural and recreation facilities. Have them explain how to get to each place from the school and what kind of service each place provides.

Teaching Tip

Some Suggestions

• Before reading passage or dialog, introduce the new vocabulary and grammatical structures. For effective visual reinforcement, use the chalkboard, flash cards, and pictures. Give many contextual examples of new words.

• Read the text. The student should not see the text at this point. Use this time as a listening comprehension exercise.

• Ask simple comprehension questions using question words such as "what," "where," "when," and "why."

• Read the text a second time, with the student reading along. As you read, tell the students to underline any unfamiliar vocabulary and expressions.

• Discuss the vocabulary and expressions the students have underlined.

• Ask more detailed comprehension questions.

Other suggestions

• Have students read the reading passage or dialog silently. Then ask basic comprehension questions.

• Have students retell the story in the passage or dialog in their own words.

• After asking detailed comprehension questions, have students ask their own detailed questions of each other.

• On another day, give a short dictation based on part of the text.

• Prepare a handout of the text with some of the vocabulary items missing (cloze-type exercise). Have students supply the missing words.

• Have students write a story modeled on the text or dialog.

• If possible, have students change story from dialog to text or vice versa.

• Do a read-and-look-up exercise. Have students read a sentence silently, then try to repeat as much of the sentence as they can without looking at it.

Advanced Level

31 Drug Abuse

1 *Write a title to the story and an ending using direct speech. Use another sheet of paper if necessary.*

_____

Jenny could hardly believe her good luck when her friend, Sally, invited her to a party that Susan Gordon was giving. Susan and her friends were at the top of school society. Jenny had always dreamed of being in their circle, and of meeting Brad, Susan's brother, on whom she had a crush.

Jenny was having a wonderful time at the party when she suddenly saw a marijuana cigarette being passed around. She whispered to Sally, "What are they smoking?"

"Oh, just a little grass," said Sally. "What's wrong with that?"

"It's just that I've never been with people who use drugs. I'm not sure it's right," replied Jenny.

"Susan's group thinks it's OK, and you'd better, too, if you want to be part of it."

Just then, Brad came up to them, holding the cigarette.

"Hey, Jenny," he said, "how about a hit?"

_____

_____

_____

Examples of Direct and Indirect Speech

(continue on another sheet of paper)

Affirmative

Pronouns must change to agree with the new sentence, and the usual sequence of tense must be followed. Examples:
Direct: John said, "I'm hungry."
Indirect: John said he was hungry.

Imperative

Use the infinitive to express a command:
Examples:
Direct: Mary told me, "Go home."
Indirect: Mary told me to go home.

Interrogrative

Express the original question in statement form: Examples:
Direct: Mary asked, "Where does John work?"
Indirect: Mary asked where John worked.

Introduce a question with "if" or "whether" if the sentence does NOT begin with a question word: Examples:
Direct: Mary asked, "Does John work here?"
Indirect: Mary asked if John worked here.

2 *Using another sheet of paper, rewrite your story using indirect speech.*

① Introduction

Discuss the following questions:

- Do you belong to a club, group, or circle of friends?
- What kind of people are in your circle of friends?
- What qualities do you look for in new friends?
- What do you and your circle of friends have in common?
- Are strangers easily accepted into your circle of friends?
- Is there a group that you would like to be part of? If so, what would you have to do to become a part of that group?
- How strong is peer pressure in your circle of friends?
- If people in your circle of friends drank alcohol, smoked cigarettes, or took drugs, what would you do about it?
- How do you feel about alcohol, tobacco, and drugs?
- Do you know anyone who takes drugs? If so, what kind? What effect do they have on people?
- How could you help a friend on drugs?
- How has drug abuse affected your community? What can be done?

② Language Activities

- Review the use of direct speech. Direct speech consists of reporting exact words of the speaker. Direct quotes are set off by quotation marks and with commas if they appear in sentences. Place all punctuation within the quotation marks. Example: "I'm not sure it's right," replied Jenny.

- Introduce new vocabulary:

hardly	grass (marijuana)	a hit (a puff)
to have a crush on someone	to whisper	
to pass around	You'd better.	

- Before handing out a copy of the story, read it to the students as a listening comprehension exercise. Then ask simple questions beginning with question words (what, where, when, why, etc.) to test the students' comprehension. Next, hand out the worksheet and read the story again while the students circle all unfamiliar vocabulary. Then explain the vocabulary.

- Discuss the story by asking students how they would continue it.

- Have students write a title and an ending to the story using direct speech.

- After the exercise has been corrected, ask for volunteers to share their stories with the class.

- On the back of the worksheet or on another piece of paper, have students rewrite their stories using indirect speech.

③ Follow-up Activity

Ask students to role-play the situations in their stories.

32 Crossword Puzzle

BAG OF TRICKS by Paul J. Hamel, © 1990 Delta Systems Co., Inc.

1 Identify the international icons in the pictures on the handout. Explain the concept of "down" and "across." Then, demonstrate how to fill in the crossword puzzle with the names for the symbols in the icons.

2 Have the students fill in the missing words. Do a few examples with the whole class.

3 Correct the answers by projecting an overhead transparency image directly onto the chalkboard where students can write the answers to the crossword puzzle.

Answers

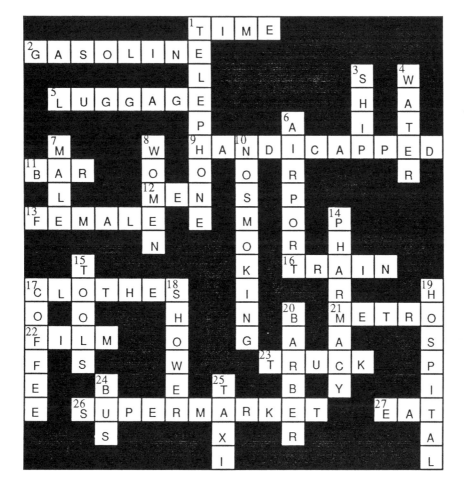

33 Giving Advice

Directions: Write your responses to the situations using modals: should, might, may, would, could.

Dear Wise One

Dear Wise One: My neighbor, who I will call Joanna, comes to my home with her three children without calling me first. She is very pleasant and friendly, but I sometimes like my privacy, and I would like to have a chance to clean my home before visitors come over. I'm afraid that if I tell her not to come without calling first, she might get angry and never come again. I don't have many friends and do not want to lose this one. What should I do? -- UNHAPPY IN NEW YORK

DEAR UNHAPPY:_____

_____

_____

_____

_____

_____

_____

Dear Wise One: I'm a woman who has found the most wonderful man in the world. He is kind, generous, and gentle. We have known each other for six months, and we spend many afternoons together. I love him very much. He says that he loves me, too, and wants to marry me. However, there is one problem--he's already married. He says that he doesn't love his wife and plans to divorce her. Every time I ask him about his divorce, he changes the subject. I don't want to wait forever. Please help me. -- LOVE SICK IN CHICAGO

DEAR LOVE SICK:_____

_____

_____

_____

_____

_____

 BAG OF TRICKS by Paul J. Hamel, © 1990 Delta Systems Co., Inc.

❶ Introduction

• Bring some newspaper articles that give advice (i.e. Dear Abby) to class.

• Read a few situations and discuss some possible solutions.

• Discuss the following questions:

1. What kind of problems are presented?
2. How often you do agree with the answers given?
3. Is the advice helpful? Why or why not?
4. What purpose do the articles serve?
5. Would you ever write for advice? Why or why not?

❷ Language Activities

• Explain polite ways to express a suggestion or give advice using modal verbs:

Should:	*You should stop* ....
	You shouldn't continue ....
Might:	*You might want to* ....
May:	*May I suggest that you* ....
	You may want to ....
Would:	*I would suggest that* ....
	If I were you, I would ....
Could:	*You could try to* ....

• Before handing out the worksheet, read the two stories to the students as a listening comprehension exercise. Then ask simple questions beginning with question words (what, where, when, why, etc.) to test the students' comprehension. Next, hand out the worksheet and read the stories again while the students circle all unfamiliar vocabulary. Then explain the vocabulary.

• Discuss possible solutions to the situations.

• Have the students write their responses to the situations using some of the modals above.

• After the exercise has been corrected, ask for volunteers to share their solutions with the rest of the class.

❸ Follow-up Activities

• Have students write an anonymous letter asking for advice.

• Distribute the letters to other students in the class.

• Ask students to answer the letters and share their responses.

34 Crossword Puzzle

ESL Advanced Level

Most of the words in the crossword puzzle contain a silent letter.

ACROSS

1. I don't drive to school; I _____ there.
4. A noise that you make on a door.
6. The first day of the weekend.
8. A part of the body at the middle of your leg.
10. Spoon, fork, _____ .
11. The past tense of CAN.
12. An important holiday.
15. The past tense of the verb THROW.
17. The ball came _____ the window and broke it.
19. He likes to _____ poems.
21. Tomatoes, potatoes, and peas are _____ .
24. A woman is beautiful; a man is _____ .
25. I _____ food at the market.

Words with Silent Letters

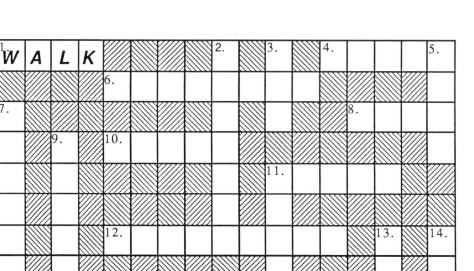

DOWN

2. People you know very well.
3. Past tense of SEE.
5. Past tense of KNOW.
7. Past tense of THINK.
9. Can you _____ my question?
11. My armchair is very _____.
13. _____ school.

14. A day in the middle of the week.
16. My _____ is 5 feet 8 inches.
18. She _____ to school by bus.
20. Something to cool your drink.
22. One, _____, three, four, ...
23. What time do you _____ dinner?

❶ Demonstrate how to do a crossword puzzle. Explain the concept of "down" and "across." Then, demonstrate how to fill in the crossword puzzle using the clues.

❷ Have the students fill in the missing words. Do a few examples with the whole class.

❸ Correct the answers by projecting an overhead transparency image directly onto the chalkboard where students can write the answers to the crossword puzzle.

Answers

Words with Silent Letters

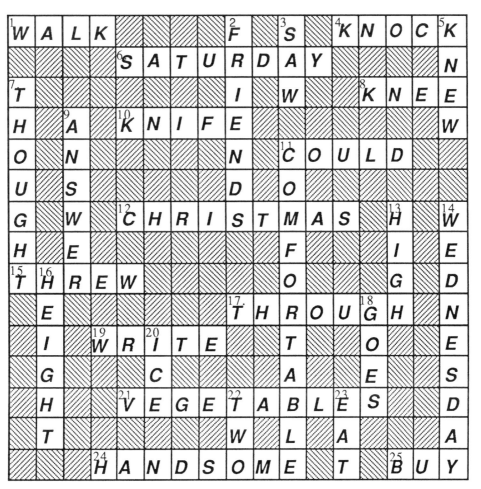

Write an ending to the story. Use the past perfect and a few of the following verbs: realize, explain, tell, think, feel, know, hear, remind.

Best of Friends

Because Joe Labrincha had transfered to Union High School in the middle of the term, he had not been able to make many friends. One of the few friends he had made was Tom Rogers, who, although friendly and bright, seemed isolated from the other students. Joe and Tom often studied and went places together after school.

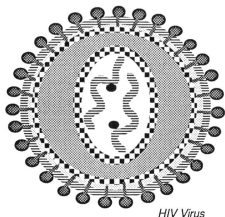

HIV Virus

One day, Joe was waiting at his locker for Tom, when Doug Cuff came up to him and said, "Joe, there's something you should know about Tom."

"What's that?" asked Joe, surprised and curious.

"Tom was in the hospital with AIDS. Everyone here at Union High knows it--that's why they stay away from him. If you keep being seen with him, they'll stay away from you, too."

Doug turned away and left abruptly as Tom came up.

"What's up?" Tom asked Joe, whose face had turned a deep red.

_____

_____

_____

_____

_____

_____

_____

1 Introduction

Discuss the following questions:

• What is AIDS? What do the letters stand for? (Acquired Immune Deficiency Syndrome)*
• How does someone get AIDS? (Through having sex and sharing needles.)
• Should everyone in this country be tested for AIDS?
• Has there been progress in stopping AIDS?
• Do you know anyone who has AIDS?
• How would you feel if you found out that one of your closest friends had AIDS?
• Would you treat him or her differently?

2 Language Activities

• Introduce new vocabulary: *transfer, term, although, isolated, locker, stay away, abruptly, "What's up?"*

• Before handing out a copy of the story, read it to the students as a listening comprehension exercise. Then ask simple questions (who, what, where, when) to test the students comprehension

• Hand out the worksheet and read the story again while the students underline unfamiliar vocabulary. Then explain the vocabulary.

• Discuss the story. Ask the students to say what they would do in this situation. Ask them to describe a conversation between Joe and Tom in which Joe asks Tom about his illness.

• Explain the use of the past perfect (or past past) tense. Show that the past perfect is used to indicate a past action that comes before another past action. See example to the right.

> **Joe heard that his friend had been in the hospital.**
>
> | Past Perfect | Past Tense ← Past | Now |
> |:---:|:---:|:---:|
> | X | X | X |
> | His friend had been in the hospital | Joe heard | |

• Practice the use of the past perfect by having the students finish the sentences below.

1. I realized that ...	3. He told me ...	5. I felt that ...	7. I heard that ...
2. She explained that ...	4. They thought that ...	6. We knew that ...	8. He reminded me ...

• Repeat the exercise above. Change the sentences to negative, then questions. Substitute the pronouns with real names.

• Have the students write an ending to the story.

1 Follow-up Activities

After correcting the students' papers, choose one of the best. Use it to prepare a handout with some of the words missing as in a cloze exercise. Read the text aloud and have the students fill in the missing words as they read along.

* You may want to refer to the U.S. Government publication "Understanding AIDS," [Publication No. (CDC) HHS-88-8404] U.S. Department of Health & Human Services, Public Health Service, Center for Disease Control, P.O. Box 6003, Rockville, MD 20850. 79

Teaching Tip

Expose students through short frequent exercises to writing that is closely related to the vocabulary, structure, and topics you have already taught. Exercises should also be varied, practical, and related to students' daily lives.

Be careful not to overwhelm students. Begin a writing program with simple exercises such as addressing envelopes and writing postcards, notes, and shopping lists. Such initial practice will give students time to learn the most commonly used words which are also the most irregularly spelled, such as pronouns, articles, prepositions, and auxiliary verbs. Once students have learned the basics, gradually build up to longer and more complex exercises.

Suggestions

• Assign writing exercises that reinforce or review previously learned material.

• When giving a writing assignment as homework, reserve the last part of the class period for writing. This will allow you to walk around the classroom to make sure everyone understands the assignment.

• When correcting the students' papers, concentrate on only serious mistakes in structure and spelling. Praise the correct use of recently taught material.

• If you find mistakes that several students are making, note them and teach a special lesson based on these mistakes.

• Include the entire class in the correcting process by copying the incorrect sentences taken from their papers onto the chalkboard, handout, or overhead transparency. Have a class discussion on how best to correct the mistakes.

• Have students rewrite their corrected exercises in a notebook.

• Keep a list of spelling errors to be used in a subsequent dictation.

General Suggestions

• Space our your best lessons and activities throughout the course to keep interest high. Don't empty your entire "bag of tricks" early on.

• Make and collect as many teaching aids (visuals, objects, handouts) as possible. Store them for future use.

80

Teacher's Notes

Teacher's Notes